Gotta Have GOD 2

AGES 2-5

Fun Devotions for Boys

HENDRICKSON PUBLISHERS   ROSE KiDZ

Lynn Marie-Ittner Klammer

Just for Mark - because sometimes the most cherished people in our lives are also the most neglected.

Gotta Have God 2 for Ages 2-5
©2014 by Lynn Marie-Ittner Klammer

Rose Kidz® is an imprint of
Rose Publishing, LLC
P.O. Box 3473
Peabody, Massachusetts 01961-3473 USA
www.hendricksonrose.com

Cover Illustrator: Dave Carleson
Interior Illustrator: Aline L. Heiser

ISBN: 978-1-58411-057-6
RoseKidz® reorder #L46964
Juvenile Nonfiction / Religion / Devotion & Prayer

Printed in the United States of America   13   11.2017.VP

TABLE OF CONTENTS

TABLE OF CONTENTS

INTRODUCTION

It's a universal truth that to be a parent is to worry...a lot.
As a mom of four I learned that early on. Even before my first child
was born, I worried about the delivery. When I brought Matthew home,
I worried if he was getting enough nourishment. As he began to crawl
and walk, I placed safety latches on the cupboards and gates over the
stairways. Every day brought new joys and new worries, but it wasn't
really until Matthew began to talk that I acquired my most important
worry. As I watched Matthew pull the garland from our just-decorated
Christmas tree one year, I wondered how to make him truly understand
what that tree signified. I worried how I would bring Matthew to not just
an understanding of our faith, but to a personal relationship with God as
well. What could I do? Where should I even start?

The devotions in this book are a good place to start. Whether you're
a worried mom, dad, grandpa, grandma or someone who simply loves
children, the true stories in this book will help you see that whether
you're sitting in church on Sunday, or just changing a diaper, God's
message is there. The stories in this book are not taken from profound,
life-altering events, but rather are based on the everyday routine moments
that we all experience. Yet it is in these seemingly unimportant snatches
of time that God's message and purpose can truly become life-changing.

With each story you will find a Bible verse, some questions for your
child to answer and a short prayer for you to share with him. A fun
activity follows each story. The stories are also related to specific themes
so you can choose which lesson you need at any given time. For example, when my two younger children smeared big sister Leahana's makeup
all over themselves (and the bathroom), it was a great opportunity to talk
about "stealing." When we made birdfeeders for our feathered friends
we discussed "stewardship." Whatever issue your child is confronted
with, you may look up a story to fit that need.

Children often are more able to comprehend the complexities of our
faith then we realize. It's in these early, formative years that we are best
able to build for them a firm foundation upon the message of God's love.
It's a message that extends beyond church and Sunday school, and teaches
that in all aspects of life – even the most mundane – **God is with them!**

CLARITY

The Bible helps me to see things better.

The discerning heart seeks knowledge.

– Proverbs 15:14

Seeing Clearly

"There's a deer outside," said Daddy.

Aaron came running. "Where? Where?" he called.

"Right there," answered Daddy, pointing out the window.

Aaron peered through the glass, trying to see the brown figure far away from the house.

"I can see it," he said, "but it's so far away! Are you sure it's a deer and not just a dog or something?"

Daddy handed Aaron a pair of binoculars and said, "Look through these. They'll help you see it better."

Aaron raised the binoculars to his eyes and moved them around until he saw the deer.

"It is a deer!" he cried excitedly. "I see it! I see it!"

Without the binoculars, Aaron couldn't tell if the brown shape he was seeing was a dog, a deer or something else. The binoculars helped Aaron to see the deer clearly.

In the same way, the Bible helps you to see things better. The Bible tells you what is the truth and how you should act. Like binoculars, the Bible makes everything clearer.

Your Turn

1. How did the binoculars help Aaron to see the deer better?

_____

_____

2. How can the Bible help you to see things better?

_____

_____

Prayer

Dear Jesus, please help me to remember that if I listen to Your words in the Bible, they will help me to see things better. Amen.

CARDBOARD BINOCULARS

Read this to your child: "The Bible teaches you about things by telling you more about them. In the same way, binoculars help you see more of something. These binoculars won't work the same way as real ones, but they're just as much fun!"

What You Need

two paper towel
tubes

crayons

glue or tape

What to Do

1. Decorate two empty paper towel tubes any way you like.

2. Place them side by side.

3. Glue the tubes together or wrap a piece of tape around both of them.

4. Use them like real binoculars!

AVOIDANCE

Jesus wants me to avoid bad things.

Avoid every kind of evil.
– 1 Thessalonians 5:22

Avoiding Trouble

"Kaylee was mean to me again," cried Adam as he ran to his mommy. "I told her to be good, just like you said, but she kept hitting me, so I ran away."

"You did the right thing," Mommy said as she hugged Adam close. "Kaylee's mommy needs to talk with her and help her to be good. Until she is, you should show her how wrong she is by staying away."

Adam didn't play with Kaylee again for a long time. Other kids didn't, either. No one likes to be hit.

Eventually, Kaylee stopped hitting. She learned how to play nicely. Adam and Kaylee were able to be friends again.

God wants you to help others be good. But when you've done all you can and they are still naughty, then sometimes you need to stay away. Pray for your friend to learn to act better.

Your Turn

1. Can you remember a time when you helped someone act nicer?

_____

_____

2. How can God help you to help someone?

_____

_____

Prayer

God, please help me to help others. But when that doesn't work, help me to know when I should stay away from them. Amen.

WHAT CAN I DO?

Read this to your child: "Jesus wants you to love and help others, but sometimes you can best help by staying away. Circle the pictures below of kids who need your help to act nicer. Tell your mommy or daddy what you would do to help."

FORETHOUGHT

I should ask God to help me before I act.

Many are the plans in a man's heart.
– Proverbs 19:21

Thinking About Cats

Daddy had just finished sweeping out the garage when he heard the children start to scream.

"Cat! Cat!" he heard.

Running inside the house, Daddy was surprised by what he saw. Alex and his big sister, Emily, were both standing up on top of the kitchen table, frightened and crying.

"He did it!" screamed Emily, pointing at Alex. "He let the cat in!"

Daddy glanced around the room to see a black cat slowly walking around and sniffing at the floor. "You let a stray cat into the house?" he asked. "Alex! How could you do such a thing!"

Daddy soon caught the cat and put it back outside, shooing it away from the house.

"Don't ever do that again," Daddy scolded Alex.

Alex felt bad. He had heard the cat meowing outside the door, so he opened the door. He didn't think about what might happen. He was lucky that the cat just wanted to sniff around! Something worse could have happened!

You should always think first before you do something. If you are unsure of what you should do, stop for a moment and ask God to help you. He is always glad to show you the right way to act.

Your Turn

1. Why did Alex let the stray cat into the house?

_____

_____

2. Would you have opened the door to the cat?

_____

_____

Prayer

God, please help me to think first before I act. I want to please You. Amen.

WHAT COULD HAPPEN?

Read this to your child: "God wants you to think first before you do something. If you are unsure of what you should do, stop for a moment and ask God to help you. He is always glad to show you the right way to act.

What do you think could have happened when Alex let the stray cat into the house? Circle the pictures of things that could have happened, and draw an X over the ones that are just silly."

STRESS

God will help my stress go away.

In my distress I called to the Lord.

– 2 Samuel 22:7

Feeling Stressed

Ben sat quietly in the doctor's office, listening as his parents asked question after question. He thought the doctor was going to just give him some medicine, but instead the doctor wanted Ben to go to the hospital for some tests.

Ben felt a scary feeling inside him. He didn't want to go to the hospital for tests. He began to cry.

Just then, Ben felt his mommy's arm slip around his shoulders. As she pulled him tight against her, he heard her whisper in his ear, "It will be okay, Ben. The tests won't hurt. And don't worry, I'll take care of you."

Suddenly, Ben felt better. He was still a little scared, but he knew his mommy and daddy were with him and loved him. He didn't need to feel so much stress about going to the hospital after all.

Just as Ben's mommy hugged him and made him feel better, God's love can help you to deal with the stress in your life. If you are ever scared, ask God to hold you safe in His care. He loves you and wants you to be happy.

Your Turn

1. How did Ben's body let him know he was feeling stress?

_____

_____

2. What can you do to make yourself feel better when you are scared?

_____

_____

Prayer

God, I know that whenever I'm scared and feeling a lot of stress that You will be there to make me feel better. Thank You for always taking such good care of me. Amen.

STOPPING STRESS

Read this to your child: "You can feel stress over lots of things. When you're scared, worried or upset, your body can act in ways that tell you you're stressed. The best way to feel better is to think about God and how much He loves you. No matter how bad things are, God is always there for you. Here are some ways to make your stress go away. Practice these with your mom or dad."

Deep Breathing

Take a breath as deep as possible, hold it for the count of 5 and then let it out slowly. Repeat.

Reading

Read your favorite Bible verse. Think of how much God loves you!

Hugging

Hug each other (or even yourself), and hold that hug for at least a count of 30.

FAITH

I can trust in God even though I cannot see Him.

Trust in the Lord forever.

– Isaiah 26:4

Seeing Sea Monkeys™

Bobby's grandparents gave him Sea Monkeys™ for Christmas. Sea Monkeys are tiny shrimp that hatch when you pour their eggs in water.

Bobby was so excited that he asked Mommy to start his Sea Monkeys for him right away. Mommy poured the water into his Sea Monkey house, and emptied the packets that came with the kit.

The next day, Mommy held the container up to the light and told Bobby to look. "There they are," she said. "There are your Sea Monkeys."

Bobby looked and looked, but he couldn't see anything. "There's nothing there!" he cried. "There are no Sea Monkeys!"

"Yes," assured Mommy, "they are tiny specks, but they're there."

"But I can't see them," said Bobby. "There's nothing there."

"Wait a few days," said Mommy. "They'll get bigger, and you'll see."

Just because you can't see something doesn't mean that it's not there. Bobby didn't believe that there were Sea Monkeys in his container because he couldn't see them. A couple of days later, however, he was surprised to see that they were there after all!

In the same way, just because you can't see God doesn't mean that He's not with you. He is there, and He's taking care of you every day.

Your Turn

1. Why didn't Bobby believe that there were Sea Monkeys in the container?

_____

_____

2. Tell about a time you didn't believe something because you couldn't see it.

_____

_____

Prayer

God, I know that even though I can't see You, You're still there all the time. Thank You for always being there. Amen.

NOW YOU SEE IT, NOW YOU DON'T

Read this to your child: "Just because you can't see something, doesn't mean it isn't there. God is like that. You can't see Him with your eyes, but you can feel Him in your heart. His love for you is so strong that He doesn't need to be seen for you to know He's there. Here's a way to find out how some things we can't see with our eyes are still there."

What You Need

magnifying glass

small items

What to Do

1. Point out to your child that there are many things around us that we can't see with our eyes.

2. Explain how the magnifying glass makes things look bigger so that we can see them.

3. Walk around the house and point out all the things that can only be seen with the magnifying glass. For example, go outside where there are many tiny creatures, stones, sand, etc., that aren't easily visible with the naked eye.

PROTECTION

God protects me.

Hide me in the shadow of your wings.

– Psalm 17:8

Daniel's Germs

"Why shouldn't I touch that?" asked Daniel as Mommy took the rattle out of his hand.

"Because it could have germs on it," answered Mommy as she washed the rattle in the sink. Daniel's little brother was sick and had been chewing on the rattle before giving it to Daniel.

"I don't see any germs," said Daniel. "What do they look like?"

"You can't see germs," said Mommy. "They're too small to see, but they're there anyway. They could make you sick like your brother."

"How can something that small hurt me?" asked Daniel. It sounded silly, but he knew that he could trust his mommy to know what was best, and protect him.

Even though you can't see something it can still hurt you. But you don't have to be afraid, because just like Mommy protected Daniel, Jesus protects you from things you cannot see.

Your Turn

1. Why did Daniel think he couldn't be hurt by germs?

_____

_____

2. Who protects you from things you cannot see?

_____

_____

Prayer

Thank You, God, for always protecting me, even from things that I can't see. Amen.

PROTECTING YOURSELF

Read this to your child: "There are many things you can do to protect yourself, but the best one is to trust God to take care of you no matter where you are or what you're doing. Here are some pictures of things that protect you. Talk with your mommy or daddy about how each of these things protects you."

FIRSTS

God makes first times special.

Whatever you do...do it all in the name of the Lord.
– Colossians 3:17

Special Times

"Look, Daddy, look!" called Peter as he pointed to his little sister, Catherine. Peter had taken the twist-tie off of the bread bag and used it to hold a ponytail at the back of Catherine's head. Peter thought she looked pretty, so he wanted Daddy to see what he had done.

"She looks very cute," said Daddy. "You know, that's the first pony-tail Catherine has ever had. Her hair was always too short to have one before. You'll always know that you were the very first to give Catherine a ponytail–and that's special."

Peter was proud of himself. He liked that he had done something for the first time with Catherine. It made him feel very special, too.

The first time you do anything can be special. Your first word, your first step, your first taste of your favorite candy–these are all special. But especially wonderful are those first things that bring you closer to God. The first time you hear a Bible story, memorize a Bible verse or learn about God's love are very special firsts. And you still have many firsts to come! God makes first times special.

Your Turn

1. Why had Catherine never had a ponytail?

_____

_____

2. What's something that you did for the first time?

_____

_____

Prayer

Thank You, God, for all the special "firsts" in my life. Please let me have many more special firsts to enjoy. Amen.

TWIST-TIE PEOPLE

Read this to your child: "God gives you many things that are special 'firsts' in your life: the first time you go to church, the first time you go to Sunday school and the first time you read the Bible for yourself are just a few of them. Here's a fun activity that may be another first for you. You can make people and other things out of twist-ties, just like Peter made a ponytail holder for Catherine. You can shape the twist-ties any way you like, but here are a few ideas."

WARMTH

Jesus' love keeps me warm, inside and out.

The peace of God...will guard your hearts and minds.
– Philippians 4:7

The Warmth of Jesus' Love

"Let me in, let me in!" cried Rachel.

"Me, too," said Brett as he pushed and prodded his way between the folds of Daddy's big, blue coat. They were waiting for Mommy to finish her shopping, and they were bored. When Daddy opened his coat and wrapped it around Rachel for a few seconds, Brett and Rachel thought it would make a fun game.

"Are you nice and warm in there?" laughed Daddy as Rachel and Brett both squirmed against him.

Brett peeked out for a moment and said, "This is our house. It's all warm and safe in here."

Brett and Rachel stayed inside Daddy's coat the whole time Mommy was shopping. They were very happy to play their game while Daddy stood still, snuggling them close.

Brett and Rachel liked being inside Daddy's coat. Up against Daddy, with his big coat wrapped around them, they felt safe. In the same way, Jesus' love can make you feel safe and warm. His arms are always wrapped around you, keeping you warm with His love and caring.

Your Turn

1. Can you think of a game that you made up when you were bored?

_____

_____

2. Whose love keeps you safe and warm?

_____

_____

Prayer

Jesus, thank You for always making me feel safe and warm when I think of You. Amen.

SAFE AND WARM

Read this to your child: "Thinking of Jesus can make you feel safe and warm, but what are some other things that make you feel that way? Here are pictures of things that make Brett feel safe and warm. Circle the ones you like best, then finish coloring the picture of your favorite one."

NAMES

God is a special name.

For in him you have been enriched in every way.

– 1 Corinthians 1:5

Names Are Special

"Maa-foo," called Sarah, "where are you?"

"Why does she always call me 'Maa-foo'?" asked Matthew with a grimace. "She knows my name is 'Matthew,' so why doesn't she call me that?"

"Well," answered Mommy, "when she was little she couldn't say 'Matthew,' and now I think it's her own special name for you."

"But it doesn't sound like it's supposed to," complained Matthew.

"I know," said Mommy, "but isn't it nicer to be called 'Maa-foo' than 'Matthew' when you know it's because she loves you so much? Don't you like it that your name is so special to Sarah?"

Matthew hadn't thought about it that way before. He decided that he liked "Maa-foo" after all.

A name is more than just something you are called. A name has meaning. It's a special word given to you with meaning and love. God's name is special, too. It's more than just a word, isn't it? His name means love, forgiveness and so many other wonderful things. "God" is a special name!

Your Turn

1. What are some things that you call by your own special names?

_____

_____

2. What do you think of when you hear the name "God"?

_____

_____

Prayer

Thank You, God, for Your special name and my special name. Amen.

THE VALUE OF A NAME

Read this to your child: "God's name is special because it reminds us of things like love and forgiveness. Your name is special, too, because it is yours. Even if other people have the same name you do, only yours was given to you for the reasons your mommy and daddy chose it for you. Here are some pictures of things that can have more than one name. How many names can you think of for each of them? You can finish coloring the pictures when you're done."

TIME

God gives me time, and ways to measure it.

There is a time for everything.

– Ecclesiastes 3:1

Stephen's Singing Clock

"That's a nice watch," said Mr. Weiss as he pointed to the watch on Stephen's arm.

Stephen smiled with joy that Mr. Weiss had noticed his new watch. He had received it from his Aunt Laura for his birthday.

"It tells me what time it is," said Stephen, "and I have a watch in my room, too."

"You do?" exclaimed Mr. Weiss.

"Yeah," answered Stephen. "My watch in my room is bigger and it even has a timer that goes off to wake me up in the morning."

"Wow," said Mr. Weiss.

"My timer sings, too," continued Stephen.

"How does it do that?" asked Mr. Weiss.

"It plays music," he answered. "My mommy says that if I learn to tell time, I'll know when things will happen, and I'll have more time for fun."

Stephen had a watch to wear on his arm, and a clock in his room to tell him the time. God gives you lots of time, and ways that you can tell time for yourself. When you learn to tell time, you can learn how to use your time well.

Your Turn

1. Can you tell time yet?

_____

_____

2. What are some ways you use your time for God?

_____

_____

Prayer

Thank You, God, for giving me time. Please help me learn to use it well. Amen.

REACTION TIME

Read this to your child: "God gives you lots of time and ways to measure it. You can measure your reaction 'time' in this activity. All you need is a dollar bill and your mom or dad to help you."

What You Need

a dollar bill

What to Do

1. Have your child stand up straight with his arm extended at about waist level.

2. Hold a dollar bill vertically with the bottom of the bill between the child's thumb and forefinger.

3. He should open his fingers, and when you drop the bill, try to catch it between his thumb and forefinger only, without moving his arm. It looks easy–but it's not! This is a good way for your child to practice hand-eye coordination.

PECULIARITIES

God made the world special.

Christle is all, and is in all.

– Colossians 3:11

Baby John's Browse Line

Whenever baby John visited his cousins, everyone had lots of fun. His cousins loved playing with him, and John enjoyed playing with them. The only thing that wasn't good was the messy house after he left.

"Why does baby John make such a mess when he's here?" asked cousin Jacob.

"John is a baby," said Mommy. "He doesn't know that he makes a mess. He is very curious, so he wants to touch and learn about things."

Mommy looked around the house and giggled. "After he leaves," she said, "I always think the house looks like it has a 'browse line.'"

Jacob laughed, too. His daddy had explained to him about a "browse line." When Jacob was in the woods with Daddy last winter, they saw how the deer ate all the brush and grass as far up as the deer could reach. Daddy told him that's called a "browse line."

"You're right," said Jacob. "Baby John pulls everything down that he can reach. I guess that's baby John's browse line."

When God made the world, he made everything special: deer browse, people eat with spoons and forks. People and animals are different, but we are all God's creation.

Your Turn

1. What is a "browse line"?

_____

_____

2. Who made the world?

_____

_____

Prayer

Thank You, God, for giving us all our own, special ways of doing things. Amen.

NATURAL ANIMALS

Read this to your child: "God made everything and everyone special. Below are some pictures of animals doing what is special to them. Look at each picture and discuss what the animal is doing, and why. Would you ever do what that animal is doing? Why, or why not?"

EXAMPLE

I can learn about love in the Bible.

In everything set them an example.

– Titus 2:7

Loving by Example

"Good night," said Mommy, tucking the blue blanket around Michael.

As Mommy started to rise off the bed to turn out the light, Michael reached out and caught her arm.

"Mommy," Michael said, "I like that you check on me when I'm sleeping."

"I'm glad," said Mommy. "I love you, and I always take care of you–even when you're asleep."

"Do you know what?" Michael asked.

"What?" Mommy answered.

"Sometimes when you're asleep," said Michael, "I come and check on you, too, to make sure you're okay."

Michael's mommy smiled as she turned out the light for bedtime.

Michael learned from his mommy that it is important to care for and love others. In the same way, you can learn from the Bible how God loves us and cares for us. The Bible gives us many examples of how we should live. The Bible says to love and care for others.

Your Turn

1. What do you do to show how much you love your mommy and daddy?

_____

_____

2. Where can you learn about loving others?

_____

_____

Prayer

Thank You, God, for teaching the world about love. Thank You for giving me parents to show me how to love others. Amen.

LOVE CARDS

Read this to your child: "In the Bible, God gives many examples of how to love others. Mommy and Daddy can show you other ways to love people, but can you think of some ways on your own to show your love for others? Make this card to show your love to someone."

What You Need

construction paper

crayons

glitter

glue

scissors

lace doilies

yarn

buttons

What to Do

1. Fold a piece of construction paper in half.

2. Fold it in half again to form a card.

3. Decorate the card any way you like with crayons, glue and glitter. Use the lace doilies to form shapes or as an edging.

4. Glue a button onto the front of the card when it opens and another onto the back of the card.

5. Cut a piece of yarn about 3" long and gently wrap an end around each button.

6. Now the person to whom you give your card has to unwrap the yarn, just like unwrapping a gift, before he or she can see your message of love inside.

CHANGE

God's love never changes.

You, O God, are my...loving God.

– Psalm 59:9-10

I Changed My Mind!

"Fine!" cried Joshua. "I'm never talking to you again!"

Joshua didn't understand why he couldn't go outside. He had been pestering Daddy to let him go, but Daddy said no. It was cold outside.

"That's fine with me," replied Daddy. "You're so grouchy today that I don't mind if you do not talk to me for the rest of the day."

"Humpf," grunted Joshua as he walked away.

A few minutes later, Joshua returned to ask again if he could go outside.

"I thought you weren't talking to me today," said Daddy.

"Grrrrr," growled Joshua as he stomped out of the room in anger.

A few minutes later, Joshua once again asked his daddy if he could go out. Again, Daddy said, "I thought you weren't talking to me."

Joshua scowled and balled his fists in frustration before yelling, "I changed my mind!"

Like Joshua, we all change our minds sometimes. Everything changes...except one thing. Do you know what that one thing is? It's God's love! Even if you do things that are bad, He will never change His mind about taking care of you. His love for you will never change.

Your Turn

1. Do you remember a time when you changed your mind about something?

_____

_____

2. What never changes?

_____

_____

Prayer

God, please help me to remember that change is just a normal part of life. Thank You for never changing Your love for me. Amen.

CHANGING COLORS

Read this to your child: "Everything in life changes, except God's love for you. His love will never change. This activity will let you change one color from another. Just follow the directions, then you can finish coloring the picture when you're done."

What You Need

glasses

water

liquid food coloring

paper towels

What to Do

1. Fill the glasses halfway with water.

2. Set the glasses on top of some paper towels.

3. One drop at a time, drip some food coloring into each glass.

4. Add different colors to each glass of water to make different colors!

SELF-HURT

God does not want me to hurt myself.

Through Christ our comfort overflows.

– 2 Corinthians 1:5

Ethan Bit Who?

"Ow!" yelled Ethan. "That hurts."

"What hurts?" asked Mommy.

"My finger hurts," said Ethan. "It hurts real bad."

"Well, why does it hurt?" asked Mommy.

"My finger hurts 'cause I bit it!" cried Ethan.

Some people worry about being hurt by others. But sometimes we hurt ourselves more than others can. If you tell yourself that you're stupid or ugly, for example, you are hurting yourself with words. In the same way, Ethan hurt himself by biting his own finger. If he had known it would hurt so much, he would never have bitten it.

The Bible teaches you a lot about taking care of others, but God also wants you to take care of yourself. God created you. Take good care of yourself so you can show God how much you love Him.

Your Turn

1. Why should you take care of yourself?

_____

_____

2. Can you remember a time when you hurt yourself? What happened?

_____

_____

Prayer

God, please help me to remember that I should take good care of myself. Help me to not do things that could hurt me. Amen.

TAKING CARE OF ME

Read this to your child: "God teaches you to not just care for others, but also to take good care of yourself. Below are some ways to take care of yourself. Which ones do you do? Have your mommy or daddy help you answer the questions."

Which of these pictures is your favorite? Why?

_____

What is the best way you can take good care of yourself?

_____

SCARING OTHERS

I should love others, not scare them.

Love one another.
– John 13:35

Scary Cow

There was a big statue of a cow in front of the grocery store. Mommy said the store put it there to remind people to buy milk because milk comes from a cow.

But Jeremy thought they put it there because it was funny.

"Moo," said Jeremy as they parked the van. "I like the cow. He's funny."

As Jeremy mooed at the cow statue, his baby sister Madison started mooing, too. That's when Jeremy got an idea. He decided to scare his baby sister.

"I'm scared," Jeremy yelled. "I'm scared that big cow is going to eat us."

Baby Madison started to cry and scream, "No cow! No cow!"

Madison got so scared that Jeremy began to feel scared, too. Before long, Jeremy was crying and screaming as much as Madison. He had meant to scare his baby sister, but Jeremy had scared himself as well!

Jeremy learned that it's not fun to scare other people. He probably felt strong and smart to be able to scare his little sister, but he wound up feeling bad in the end. It's not right to scare other people. God wants us to love and protect others, not scare them.

Your Turn

1. Why did Jeremy say he was afraid of the cow?

_____

_____

2. Have you ever tried to scare someone? Why or why not?

_____

_____

Prayer

God, please help me to remember that it's not nice to scare other people. Amen.

WHAT'S SCARY?

Read this to your child: "God says it is not right to scare others. He wants us to comfort, not scare, each other. Below are some pictures of things that are scary, and ways to deal with them. Draw a line from the scary picture to the picture that shows what you would do."

EXCUSES

God wants me to tell the truth and not make excuses.

Men are without excuse.

– Romans 1:20

Baby Hannah

"Mommy, Mommy, wait until you hear what Hannah did!" cried Joseph.

Joseph had found his little sister in the bathroom, smearing soapy water all over the counter and walls.

Hannah stood in front of Mommy while Joseph stood behind Hannah, waiting for her to explain her naughty behavior. Hannah said nothing.

"Hannah," said Mommy, "I want you to tell me what you did."

Hannah said nothing, but she tilted her head, fluttered her eyelashes and tried her best to look very cute.

"Hannah, looking cute won't help," said Mommy. "Tell me what you did."

Hannah still said nothing, but this time she held up her thumb to Mommy, then put it in her mouth and sucked on it like a little baby. After a few moments, Hannah pulled her thumb out, looked straight at Mommy and said, "I'm the baby."

Hannah thought that being the baby of the family would keep her from getting into trouble. She thought that she could do whatever she wanted because she had the excuse of being too young to know better. But there are no excuses for bad behavior. God wants you to be good. Even when you aren't, you should always tell the truth instead of making excuses.

Your Turn

1. Why did Hannah think she could get away with being bad?

_____

_____

2. Have you ever used an excuse to get out of trouble?

_____

_____

Prayer

God, please help me to remember that there's no good excuse for being bad. Amen.

SOAPY MESS

Read this to your child: "God teaches that there's no good excuse for being bad. You should try to be good all the time. Hannah used the soap in the bathroom for bad things, but sometimes soap can be used for fun. Here's a recipe for making bubbles out of soap."

What You Need

¼ cup liquid dish detergent

½ cup water

dipping items
(see below)

What to Do

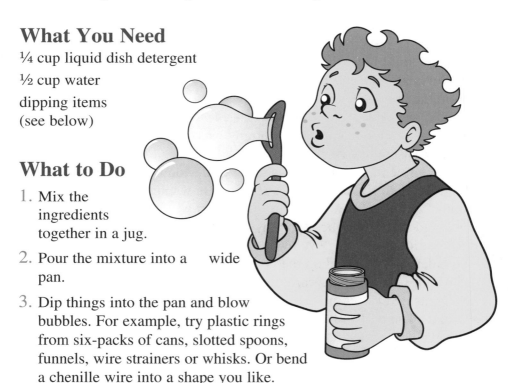

1. Mix the ingredients together in a jug.

2. Pour the mixture into a   wide pan.

3. Dip things into the pan and blow bubbles. For example, try plastic rings from six-packs of cans, slotted spoons, funnels, wire strainers or whisks. Or bend a chenille wire into a shape you like.

LYING

God wants me to tell the truth.

Do not lie to each other.
– Colossians 3:9

Nicholas Lies

"Who is it?" asked Mommy. She had locked the door to her bedroom so that she could have time alone. But now she was hearing a knock.

"Who is it?" she asked again.

From the other side of the door came Nicholas's soft voice. "It's me...Nick," he said.

Nicholas wanted to see what Mommy was doing. He didn't like when Mommy wasn't where he could see her.

"You can't come in right now," answered Mommy. "I'm busy."

Nicholas didn't like Mommy's answer. He wanted to get into the bedroom...but how? How could he get Mommy to let him in? Then he remembered that sometimes Mommy would let his big brother Andrew into the bedroom with her even when she wouldn't let anyone else in.

Nicholas softly rapped on the door again, but this time when Mommy asked who it was, Nicholas carefully answered, "It's Andrew!"

Nicholas lied to get into Mommy's bedroom, but it didn't work. He should have just told Mommy that he needed to be with her. Mommy would have understood. God never wants you to lie. You should always tell the truth.

Your Turn

1. How did Nicholas try to get into the bedroom?

_____

_____

2. Have you ever lied to get what you want?

_____

_____

Prayer

God, please help me to remember that it's not okay to lie, even if it will get me what I want. Amen.

FINGER PUPPETS

Read this to your child: "God doesn't like when you lie. He wants you to tell the truth. Below are some ideas for finger puppets. Make them, then act out some stories with Mommy or Daddy about being honest."

What You Need

plastic or cotton gloves

sewing supplies

pens

Velcro

felt

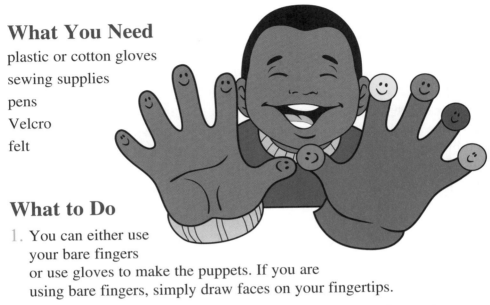

What to Do

1. You can either use your bare fingers or use gloves to make the puppets. If you are using bare fingers, simply draw faces on your fingertips.

2. If you'd like to be more creative, sew faces on cotton gloves. An easy way to do that is to sew Velcro on felt parts so you can change the puppet's face as desired.

3. Another way to make the puppets is to draw faces on plastic gloves.

4. For this activity, focus less on designing the puppets and more on giving the child plenty of opportunity to act out honest and dishonest situations.

TENACITY

God wants me to try hard and not give up.

What I have vowed I will make good.

– Jonah 2:9

Timothy's Fall

Late at night, after his brother and sisters were asleep, Timothy's favorite thing to do was slip quietly into bed beside Mommy. He would climb up onto the bed, and Mommy would snuggle him close.

One night, however, Mommy didn't hold quite tight enough to Timothy, and he fell off the edge of the bed. Fortunately, Mommy kept a pillow on the floor next to the bed – just in case – so Timothy wasn't hurt. In fact, he was sleeping so well that he never even woke up! He just kept sleeping, and eventually slid his way under the bed while he slept. When he woke up there the next morning, he was very surprised!

Sometimes you will end up in a difficult place. Timothy ended up under the bed, but there are other difficult places you could be. Maybe you've been with a friend who isn't playing nicely. Or perhaps you are trying to learn to tie your shoes and you can't seem it to get it right.

God doesn't want you to give up. You might need to ask for help or you might just need to practice at what you're doing. Whatever it takes, know that God will be proud of you if you keep trying and not give up.

Your Turn

1. Have you ever had to find your way back from somewhere you didn't want to be?

_____

_____

2. Have you ever given up on something? Why?

_____

_____

Prayer

God, please help me to remember that I can get to where I want to go if I just keep trying. Amen.

STAY TO THE COURSE

Read this to your child: "God doesn't want you to give up, even when things are hard. If you remember to keep trying, you can get where you want to be. Try to find your way through the maze to get to the mommy's bed."

CHARM

I should obey my parents.

The unfaithful are destroyed by their duplicity.

– Proverbs 11:3

Charming Christopher

Christopher knew he was cute. Daddy told him so. Grandma and Grandpa told him so. And Mommy certainly told him that he was.

Sometimes, when Christopher did something naughty, he would give a little smile, and Mommy would give him a hug instead of a scolding.

One night, when it was way past Christopher's bedtime, Mommy warned him that if he didn't go to bed he was going to get into trouble. Christopher scrambled up onto Mommy and Daddy's bed, sat down in the middle and said, "I sleep here."

"No, Christopher," answered Mommy gently. "You have to sleep in your own bed tonight."

"I'm not going to sleep in my bed," insisted Christopher.

"Why do you say that?" Mommy asked.

Christopher thought for a moment, then replied, "I'm going to charm Daddy, and I'm going to charm you!"

Christopher thought that he could use his cuteness to charm his parents into letting him sleep with them, but that wasn't the right thing to do. God does not want you to use your parents' love to get what you want. God wants you to obey your parents, because that's the right thing to do.

Your Turn

1. Have you ever used charm to get something you wanted?

_____

_____

2. Why is using charm in this way a bad thing?

_____

_____

Prayer

God, please help me to be grateful for being loved. I'll try to never use my parents' love to get my own way. Amen.

FLOWER POT FLOWERS

Read this to your child: "God doesn't want you to use your parents' love as a way to get what you want, as Christopher did. Here is something fun you can make that will charm people in a good way."

What You Need

craft sticks or plastic drinking straws

plain paper or construction paper

crayons

scissors

tape or glue

What to Do

1. Cut out a flower shape from paper.

2. Color it or decorate it the way you want.

3. Tape or glue the flower onto the craft stick, making sure you keep your flower at the top half of the stick.

4. Push your Flower Pot Flower into someone's plant (ask if it is okay first). Every time they water their plant, they'll see it and be charmed by your thoughtfulness.

CONSIDERATION

I need to be considerate of others.

Do...only what is helpful for building others up.
– Ephesians 4:29

Nicole's Kisses

It was a wonderful Christmas party! Patrick and his little sister, Nicole, loved this party each year. It had fancy food, pretty decorations and lots of people. One of Patrick's favorite things to do was watch movies in the movie room, but this Christmas Nicole was being naughty.

As Patrick tried to watch the movie, Nicole kept leaning over and kissing him on the cheek. Then she started to give kisses to the other people in the room, too.

Patrick ran to Daddy and told him how Nicole was kissing everybody. "She's being bad," said Patrick. "Make her stop, or make her leave."

Daddy knelt down next to Nicole. "It is nice to show you love people," he told Nicole, "but not when they are trying to watch a movie. You need to be considerate of others."

Kissing and hugging aren't the only ways to love others. You also can show people you love them by being considerate. Obeying the rules, letting others go first and sharing are all ways to show others you love them. God wants you to love others, but only in considerate ways.

Your Turn

1. What was right about Nicole's kisses? What was wrong?

_____

_____

2. Are you always considerate of others?

_____

_____

Prayer

God, please help me to remember to be considerate of others. Amen.

CONSIDERATE LOVE

Read this to your child: "God wants you to love others, but you should show your love in ways that are considerate of others. There are ways to show your love that make people happy. Circle the pictures below that are considerate ways to show your love, and draw a square around the ones that some people might not like."

POWER

Jesus is more powerful than anything else.

The joy of the Lord is your strength.

– Nehemiah 8:10

The Powerful Wind

It was a very windy day. It was so windy, in fact, that the front door suddenly blew open because it wasn't closed tightly!

As Mommy ran to the door to close it, William said, "The wind just wanted to get in, Mommy."

William was afraid that the wind might blow the door open again. Mommy explained to him that once the door was tightly shut, the wind wasn't powerful enough to blow it open.

Wind can be powerful. William was afraid of the wind because it seemed so strong, but the door protected him.

God is like that big, strong door. When your faith isn't strong enough, the evil wind can blow in. But if your faith is strong, you are protected from the bad wind. God protects you from evil. He is more powerful than anything, even a door!

Your Turn

1. Why was the wind able to blow the door open at first, but not after Mommy closed it tight?

_____

_____

2. Who is like a door and protects you from bad things?

_____

_____

Prayer

Thank You, God, for being so powerful that I feel protected all the time. Amen.

PAPER KITE

Read this to your child: "God can protect you from everything–even the wind when it's blowing very strong. Here's something that you can do to control the wind a little, and make it fun."

What You Need

8½" x 11" paper

tissue paper

string or yarn

crayons

glue or tape

scissors

What to Do

1. Decorate the paper with crayons.

2. Starting at the top of the paper, roll it down loosely to make a tube shape with the picture on the outside.

3. Carefully manipulate one end of the tube to be more narrow (like a funnel). This doesn't have to be perfect, but the kite will work better if one end is tapered.

4. Cut the tissue paper into three 1" x 8" strips and attach them to the pointed end of the funnel with tape or glue.

5. Attach a 3-foot long string or piece of yarn to the wide end of your funnel, and you're ready to fly your kite!

REJUVENATION

God's love and care make people new.

The Lord is…abounding in love.

– Psalm 103:8

The "New" Car

The car was old and orange. Its windows were all open, and there was brown yucky stuff on it called "rust." The "new" car couldn't even run by itself. Daddy had to tie it to the truck and pull it home.

This was not at all how Anthony thought a new car would look. He thought it would be beautiful!

"What a piece of junk," Anthony said as Daddy stopped the car in the driveway. "Why'd you buy this car? It's just a piece of junk!"

"That car may look like junk now," said Mommy, "but just wait until Daddy fixes it up." Mommy explained how the car had been left sitting outside for a long time with no one to care for it, but now that they had it, the car would be just fine.

God takes care of us like Anthony's daddy was taking care of the old car. People who don't have God in their lives can be like the old car. They can be all beat up by life and in need of attention and love. But once God comes into their lives, His love and care fixes them all up. God makes people "new" again!

Your Turn

1. Could the car be fixed up to look as good as new?

_____

_____

2. How do you think God's love makes someone's life new?

_____

_____

Prayer

Thank You, God, for Your love and care that makes us new. Amen.

COLOR THE CAR

Read this to your child: "When people are feeling sad or sick, God can make a difference. Just like Daddy could fix the car to be like new again, God can fix people. Below is a picture of the car that Anthony's daddy bought. You can't see it? Just color in the letter C and you'll soon see the car."

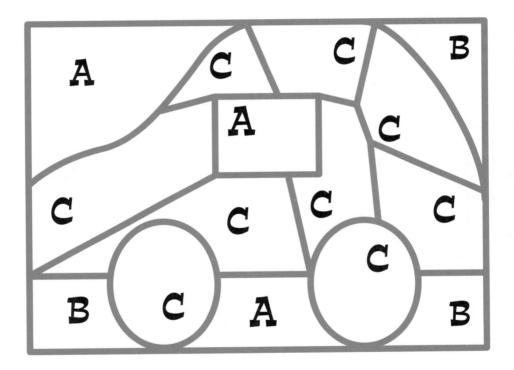

SYMBOLS

Symbols remind me of God.
Let us acknowledge the Lord.
– Hosea 6:3

Mrs. Heart

David loved Sunday school. In fact, it was his favorite time of the week.

"When can I see Mrs. Heart again?" asked David. "How long is it until Sunday?"

"Who is Mrs. Heart?" Mommy asked.

"Mrs. Heart is my Sunday school teacher," answered David.

"No, she's not," said Mommy. "You know very well that your teacher's name is Mrs. Zehnder."

"Oh, I know," said David, "but I call my teacher 'Mrs. Heart' because I love her so much."

David called his teacher Mrs. Heart because, to him, a heart was a symbol of love and he loved his teacher. Just as a heart was a symbol of love for David, other things can be symbols of God's love for you. Pictures of a dove, cross or rainbow are just a few of the things that can remind you of God and His love for you. They are things that can help you remember how important God is in your life.

Your Turn

1. Can you think of some symbols in your life?

_____

_____

2. What symbol reminds you of God?

_____

_____

Prayer

God, thank You for giving me lots of symbols to remind me of how important You are in my life. Amen.

SYMBOLS OF JESUS

Read this to your child: "There are many symbols to help remind you of God. Several are below. Finish coloring them, then talk about what they mean."

Symbol Explanations

The cross reminds us of Jesus' sacrifice in the crucifixion.

The fish symbolizes salvation in Christ through water baptism.

The dove is a symbol of the Holy Spirit, divine inspiration and peace.

The lamb reminds us of Jesus, who is often referred to as the sacrificial lamb of God.

Churches are a symbol of joining with other believers to worship God.

Rainbows symbolize God's promise to always be with us.

DIFFERENCES

God made me different.

In all things God works...good.
– Romans 8:28

Bird Love

Thud!

The sudden sound of a bird flying into the living room window startled Ryan. "What was that?" he asked.

"It's okay," Mommy replied. "A bird hit the window, but he'll be okay."

Mommy pointed to where the bird sat in the grass, breathing heavily.

"He's just stunned," she said. "In a few minutes he'll be fine."

"Can I go outside?" asked Ryan, eager to get closer to the bird.

"Yes, just don't get too close," answered Mommy.

"Can I pet the bird?" Ryan asked. "I'll be very careful."

"No, I don't think that's a good idea, honey."

"Can I kiss the little birdie?" asked Ryan, smiling. "I love him."

"No, that wouldn't be good either. The bird would get scared then."

Ryan wanted to love the bird and be nice to it, but petting it or kissing it could have been hurtful to the bird.

Showing love is different for different things. Everyone, and everything, has different needs. If you want to show love, then you must consider those needs first. In the same way, God knows you and your special needs. He knows what is best for you.

Your Turn

1. What do you need when you are hurt?

_____

_____

2. Who knows what is best for you?

_____

_____

Prayer

God, I'm glad You know all the ways that I'm different. Thank You for loving all those special things about me. Amen.

TISSUE BUTTERFLY

Read this to your child: "God made you special. That's why the things you like and need are a little different from other people. God loves all the special things about you. Here's something Ryan could have made to help the birds stop flying into the window. With this tissue butterfly hanging against the glass, birds will be able to see that they can't fly there, and won't hurt themselves."

What You Need

facial tissue

old newspapers

clothespins or chenille wire

markers

string

What to Do

1. Place a tissue (white works best) on top of some newspaper (to protect the tabletop) and decorate the tissue with markers. Simply holding the marker tip to the tissue will produce color. If you push or rub, the tissue may tear. Allow to dry.

2. Gather the tissue in the center and cinch it with a clothes-pin (or a chenille wire).

3. With the handles of the clothespin facing up, you'll see that the handles can appear to be antennae. If you use a pipe cleaner, you'll need to make sure the two ends point up to form the antennae.

4. Thread a string through the spring of the clothespin (or around the center/body of the pipe cleaner) and hang in your window.

REALITY

God gave me parents to teach me.

He commanded our forefathers to teach their children.
– Psalm 78:5

This World

"Is that in this world?" Tyler asked, pointing to a cartoon that he was watching on TV.

"Why does he always ask that?" Tyler's big brother, Jake, asked. "Can't he tell that's a cartoon and not real?"

"Well," explained Daddy, "Tyler is little, so he's still learning many things you already know. Everything is new to him! When he sees a cartoon on TV, it's hard for him to know if it's real or not real."

"Yeah, but he asks about everything," said Jake, "even stuff he should know is real, like trees and birds."

What you see on TV and in pictures can seem real. It can be difficult to know what is real and what is pretend. That's one of the reasons God gave you parents. They will help you understand what is real, and what isn't. The next time you are confused about whether something is real, ask your parents and listen to what they teach you. Also, pray and ask God to help you understand. Your parents and God want you to learn and grow smarter about the world.

Your Turn

1. Do you ever have a hard time knowing if something you see on TV is real or not?

_____

_____

2. Who can you ask if you are not sure if something is real?

_____

_____

Prayer

God, please help me to know what is real and what isn't. Amen.

WHAT'S REAL?

Read this to your child: "Not everything you see on TV or hear is real. That's why it's important to learn from God, and your parents, what is real and what isn't. Below are some pictures of things that animals do. In each pair, one of the things is real, and one isn't. Circle the picture that is real in each pair, then finish coloring the pictures."

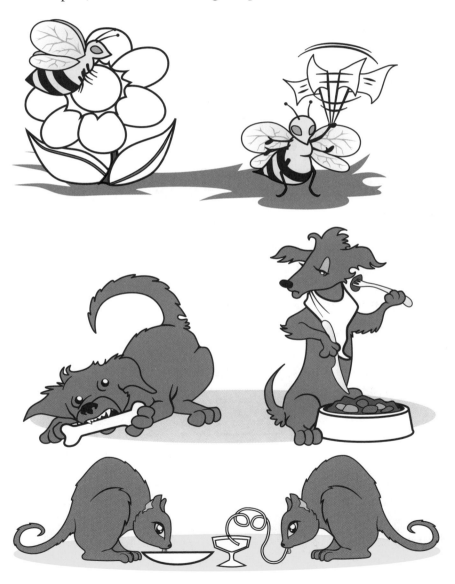

#

Only God has power over life and death.

Salvation comes from the Lord.

– Jonah 2:9

Poor Kitty

One day as Henry rode in Mommy's car, he saw an orange cat lying at the side of the road. The next day, Henry watched as he passed the cat again. It didn't move. It just lay there very still as they drove past.

"Why is the kitty lying on the side of the road?" Henry asked his mommy.

"That cat died," Mommy explained. "Sometimes animals get hit by cars because the cars drive so fast that it's difficult for the animal to get out of the way in time."

Henry thought about what Mommy had said. He couldn't understand why no one had taken the cat to the doctor.

"Can we take the kitty to the animal hospital?" Henry asked.

Mommy reached for Henry's hand. "No," she said gently, "it is too late to help that cat. Nothing will bring it back to life now."

Doctors and hospitals can sometimes help when people or animals are hurt, but not always. Only God can bring a person back to life. He brought Jesus back to life after He died on the cross. God did that for us so we could live with Him in heaven forever.

Your Turn

1. Why couldn't the hospital help the cat?

_____

_____

2. Who died and rose again so you could live in heaven?

_____

_____

Prayer

Dear God, I'm glad that You have power over life and death. I want to live with You in heaven someday. Amen.

EGG SHELL GARDEN

Read this to your child: "Only God has power over life and death, but you can do something that helps to create life. Follow the directions below, and before you know it, you'll have something living on your windowsill!"

What You Need

six eggs

egg carton

seed

potting soil

water

a sunny spot

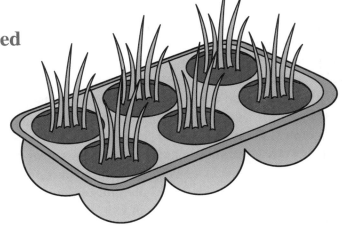

What to Do

1. Save six eggshells, breaking off no more than half of the shell.

2. Cut the egg carton in half and place the half-shells in it.

3. Fill the shells with soil.

4. Press in some seed (grass seed works well).

5. Water the soil.

6. Place the carton in a sunny place. Check once or twice a day to make sure the soil stays damp.

BODY

My body is a gift from God.

Your body is a temple of the Holy Spirit.

– 1 Corinthians 6:19

The Ticklish Fan

James giggled as the air blew his hair back from his face. The wind was strong, warm and loud, but James loved it. He could feel his hair drying as the air blew through his hair and tickled his face and neck.

"Do it again, do it again," James pleaded when Mommy turned off the blow dryer. "I want more. Blow the ticklish fan on me more!"

Mommy stopped, but now she poured some sweet-smelling lotion and rubbed it into James's hands. It felt squishy and cool as Mommy smoothed it over his skin. When Mommy was done with that, she brushed James's hair. He loved the pull of the brush as it softly glided through his hair. It felt so good, in fact, that James almost fell asleep!

James loved to have Mommy do things that felt good on his body. Our bodies are gifts from God. It is good to enjoy your body and take care of it.

Your Turn

1. How do you take care of your body?

_____

_____

2. Who gave us our bodies?

_____

_____

Prayer

God, thank You for giving me such a wonderful body so I can feel so good. Amen.

FEELING GOOD

Read this to your child: "God wants you to feel good and enjoy the body He has given you. Here's a picture of James feeling good for you to finish coloring any way you like."

PLANNING

Planning ahead helps me to live as God wants.

Make the most of every opportunity.

– Colossians 4:5

The Porcupine Tree

"I want to save this for the birdies," Freddie said as he carried the earthworm in his hands. I'll put it in their nest in the porcupine tree."

"The porcupine tree?" Mommy asked. "Why do you call the pine tree the 'porcupine tree'?"

Freddie giggled and said, "Because it pricks my fingers when I touch it."

"That's a good name for it," Mommy agreed, "but I don't think you should put anything in the nest."

"Why not?" asked Freddie.

"Because the birds have already finished growing up," Mommy explained. "The summer is over, and they've all flown away to where it's warm. They don't use that nest anymore."

"Oh," said Freddie, thinking. "Well, maybe I can save it until next year."

Everything and everyone should plan for the future. Some birds plan for the coming winter by flying to where it's warmer. Freddie was planning ahead by saving the worm for the birds until spring. As a young Christian, you plan your life by learning as much about God as you can, so that you can live your life the way He wants.

Your Turn

1. Why did Freddie call the pine tree a "porcupine" tree?

_____

_____

2. What are some things you do each day to plan for the future?

_____

_____

Prayer

God, please help me to plan for my life, so that I can live as You want. Amen.

DIVING DROPPER

Read this to your child: "God wants you to plan for your life so that you will be happy and live the way He teaches you to live. If you plan carefully for this activity, you will be able to control the diving dropper."

What You Need

glass jar
medicine dropper
balloon
rubber band
scissors

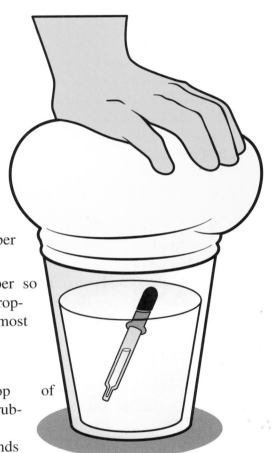

What to Do

1. Fill a jar with water (it should be large enough that the dropper will float freely at the top).

2. Put enough water in the dropper so that it floats on top. The dropper should be so full that it almost sinks, but not quite.

3. Cut the neck off of a balloon.

4. Stretch the balloon over the top   of the jar, sealing it shut. Use a rubber band to hold it secure, or just hold it tight with your hands before the next step.

5. Press lightly on top of the balloon, and you'll see the dropper descend into the jar. When you release the pressure, the dropper will float back to the top. You control the diving dropper!

Note: This is a messy activity as water will seep out of the jar.

IMAGINATION

God wants me to use my imagination in only good ways.

It is the Lord's purpose that prevails.

– Proverbs 19:21

Indian Stripes

"Look, Daddy," said Eddie, holding out his arm for Daddy to see.

"Oh, look at that," said Daddy, "I guess those cuffs made lines on your arm." Eddie's pajamas had elastic in the sleeve cuffs, and they had left a light mark behind.

"No," answered Eddie, "those aren't lines. They're Indian stripes. Zack told me so." Zack was Eddie's older brother. Zack had a big imagination.

"They do look like stripes," laughed Daddy.

With Zack's help, Eddie began to pinch and scratch himself to make more "Indian stripes" on himself. When Daddy saw what they were doing, he didn't laugh any longer. Daddy told Zack and Eddie to stop hurting Eddie's skin.

Zack and Eddie had good imaginations, but they used their imaginations in bad ways. God gave you your imagination. He wants you to use it for fun and good things. God doesn't want you to use your imagination to hurt yourself or others.

Your Turn

1. What are some bad ways you've used your imagination?

_____

_____

2. How can you use your imagination to help God?

_____

_____

Prayer

God, thank You for giving me an imagination. Please help me to remember to use my imagination in only good ways. Amen.

CHANGING COLORS

Read this to your child: "God wants you to use your imagination in good ways. Here's an activity where you can use your imagination and have fun with the imaginations of others."

What You Need

two containers of white frosting

food coloring

sugar cookie dough

What to Do

1. Color one container of frosting pink, and the other brown.

2. Bake a batch of cookies.

3. Frost half of the cookies with the pink frosting and the other half with the brown frosting.

4. Now taste the cookies. Do they taste the same?

5. Have others taste the cookies without telling them you colored the frosting. You will find that most people think they taste chocolate and strawberry in the frosting instead of just vanilla. Why? Because vision and imagination can affect your other senses, including what you taste.

GOSSIP

I should be a good friend by not gossiping.

Avoid godless chatter.
– 2 Timothy 2:16

Gossip Hurts

"Jenny says her dad likes to sit in his chair at night and watch TV," said Michael on the playground one day. "She says he's lazy."

Michael's friends all giggled and jumped up and down saying, "Lazy, lazy, Jenny's dad is lazy."

They were having so much fun that they didn't notice Jenny walk up. "My dad's not lazy!" she screamed. "Stop it! Stop saying that!"

As Michael watched Jenny run away crying, he felt sad inside. He didn't mean to make fun of Jenny's dad. He just wanted to have the other kids' attention for a while, and make them laugh. Now Jenny was upset all because of him.

Jenny shouldn't have said something so mean about her dad, but even though she did, Michael shouldn't have repeated it. When people trust you with their thoughts and feelings, God wants you to keep them to yourself. When you tell others such things just for fun, or to be hurtful, then it's gossiping. Gossiping is wrong.

Your Turn

1. Why do you think Michael told the other kids what Jenny had said?

_____

_____

2. Have you ever gossiped about someone or something? Why did you do it?

_____

_____

Prayer

God, please help me to be a good friend to others, and never gossip. Amen.

MAKING UP

Read this to your child: "God doesn't want you to gossip, because that can be hurtful to people. God only wants you to be loving and kind to others. Michael hurt Jenny's feelings when he told the others that her dad was lazy, but after he told her he was sorry, they made up and were good friends again. Here is a picture of Jenny and Michael especially for you to finish coloring."

JUDGMENT

I should not judge others.

Forgive as the Lord forgave you.

– Colossians 3:13

The Evil Red Car

Bang!

Justin heard the sound of something as it hit the side of the van. When he looked out the window, he saw a woman had hit the van with her car door.

"Mommy," Justin said, "that car just hit our van!"

"What car?" asked Mommy.

Justin pointed at the red car next to them as the driver walked away.

"Why would she just walk away?" Mommy wondered aloud.

"Because she's evil!" Justin answered. Justin knew the word 'evil' meant something bad. "That's the evil red car!"

"Now Justin," said Mommy, "she may not have meant to hit our van. It could have been an accident. You shouldn't judge the lady for what she did by calling her 'evil'."

Justin thought that just because the lady in the red car had hit the van, she must be evil. But that may not have been the case, as Mommy said.

It is wrong to judge people if you do not know all of the facts. Only God knows what's really in people's hearts and why they do the things that they do. We are to forgive, just like God forgives us.

Your Turn

1. Why do you think the lady hit the van with her car door?

_____

_____

2. Did you ever judge someone without knowing all the facts?

_____

_____

Prayer

God, help me to remember that only You can judge people and what they do. Amen.

WHY?

Read this to your child: "God doesn't want you to judge other people. Only God really knows why people do what they do, and only He should judge others. Here are some things that people sometimes do. Talk with Mommy or Daddy about why you think the people in the pictures did what they did."

ENCOURAGEMENT

When I encourage others I show God's love.

Build each other up.

– 1 Thessalonians 5:11

Kyle's Kite

"You can do it!" screamed Johnny to his brother, Kyle, as they flew their kites in the front yard.

The wind tugged and shoved at Kyle's kite, suddenly pushing it up into the air. But then just as quickly, it slammed down into the ground.

"Why doesn't the wind just keep it up there?" cried Kyle, falling to his knees. He wanted to give up, but Johnny wouldn't let him.

"Just try again," Johnny said each time Kyle's kite fell. "I know you can do it if you just try one more time."

It took many "tries," but with Johnny's encouragement, Kyle soon had his kite flying overhead.

Johnny was showing how to be a Christian when he encouraged Kyle. God wants you to encourage others and make them feel good. When you show people love by encouraging them, you are passing along the love that God gives you.

Your Turn

1. Have you ever encouraged someone?

_____

_____

2. How does encouragement show God's love?

_____

_____

Prayer

God, please help me to remember that I should encourage others whenever I can. Amen.

BLOWING POM-PONS

Read this to your child: "God wants you to encourage others, just like Johnny encouraged Kyle. It's a wonderful way to help people when they're having a hard time. Kyle couldn't understand why the wind wouldn't keep his kite in the air. Wind can be hard to understand, but here's an activity where it's easy to understand how your pom-pon blows in the wind."

What You Need
cardboard
yarn
scissors

What to Do

1. Cut two 2-inch diameter circles out of cardboard.

2. Cut a ½ to ¾-inch circle out of the middle of each cardboard circle.

3. Press the two cardboard circles together so they match up.

4. Tie your two circles together by wrapping the end of the yarn through the center of the circles and knotting them.

5. Continue to thread the yarn through the center of the cardboard circles and around the outside (keeping the yarn snug but not tight).

6. Go around and around until your circle is completely covered in yarn and you can no longer get the yarn through the center. The more yarn you use, the fuller the pom-pon will be.

7. Ease the two cardboard circles slightly apart and slide one of the blades of your scissors in between.

8. Cut all around the diameter, staying in the groove. Be careful not to disturb the yarn as you cut.

9. Carefully remove the two cardboard circles and tie the center of your cut yarn with another piece of string (about 8 inches long).

10. Now simply fluff your pom-pon and hang it in the wind to watch it blow!

COLORS

God made many colors.

In the beginning God created the heavens and the earth.
– Genesis 1:1

Grass Green

"I need green," said Sam, digging through the bag of crayons. His little sister, Elizabeth, handed him a crayon, but Sam just shook his head.

"Not that green!" Sam yelled. "I want grass green."

"That is green!" Elizabeth hollered right back at him.

"No, it's not," cried Sam as he looked from the crayon to the blade of grass in his hand. "It's not the same."

Sam looked through the whole bag of crayons, but no matter how many green crayons he found, none of them looked exactly the same as the grass.

We live in a colorful world. God created our beautiful world. There are so many colors in our world that we cannot even count them! We should be thankful to God for giving us such a wonderful place to live.

Your Turn

1. What is your favorite color?

_____

_____

2. Who made the world?

_____

_____

Prayer

Thank You, God, for making such a beautiful, colorful world for me to live in. Amen.

A COLORFUL WORLD

Read this to your child: "God made all the different colors in this world. There are so many that you could never even see or name them all. To find out, go outside and pick a few blades of grass. Line them up side by side. See how they are each green? If you look closely, you will notice that even though they are all green, there are different shades of green in each blade. You can see this in many other things, too: bark, stones, leaves, flowers and so on. There are as many colors as there are things in this world. What a beautiful, colorful world God made for us! Here's a picture for you to finish coloring with your colorful crayons."

MEANINGS

Everything God gives has a special meaning.

It will...achieve the purpose for which I sent it.
– Isaiah 55:11

What Does That Mean?

"Why do we call Sarah 'Boo-Beara'?" asked Adam. He noticed that they usually called his baby sister "Boo-Beara" instead of her real name, Sarah.

"When Sarah was a baby," answered Daddy, "she used to get a lot of boo-boos. So Aunt Leah called her the boo-boo baby. As she got a little older, it changed to 'boo-boo-beara.'"

Later that same day, Adam asked, "Why does the dog bark when he hears someone in the yard?"

"Because his bark means that he sees someone and he wants us to know," explained Daddy.

"Why do all the cars stop at that red sign on the corner of our road?" Adam asked later.

"Because that sign means 'stop,'" said Daddy.

Adam had a lot of questions about why things are the way they are, but that's how he was learning their meanings. There is a meaning for everything God has created in this world. See how many you can learn!

Your Turn

1. Can you think of some things for which you don't know the meaning?

_____

_____

2. Who created the world?

_____

_____

Prayer

God, thank You for all the special things in the world. Please help me to learn their special meanings. Amen.

COMMON MEANINGS

Read this to your child: "God gives special meaning to everything in the world. Finish coloring the pictures below and then decide what they each mean. Some even have more than one meaning."

CONTROL

I should control my actions.

If you falter in times of trouble, how small is your strength!
– Proverbs 24:10

Losing Control

Austin loved bubble gum. He loved the way it tasted sweet, how it was chewy and especially how he could blow bubbles...well, almost. Austin tried and tried to blow bubbles with his gum, but no matter how hard he tried, the best bubble he could make was a very tiny one.

One day when Austin and Mommy were shopping, he asked for some gum to practice his bubble blowing.

"Well, okay," said Mommy, "but be careful. Keep the gum in your mouth."

As Mommy shopped, Austin carefully formed his gum inside his mouth and pursed his lips to make a bubble. He blew, and blew, and blew...and out popped his gum, right onto the floor of the store. Mommy and Austin were so embarrassed!

Austin had lost control of his gum, even though he believed he was able to keep it in his mouth. Lots of things in life are like that. If you don't control your actions, you could do something to hurt others or yourself. You may not always be able to control your actions, but God and your parents expect you to try.

Your Turn

1. How could losing control hurt somebody or something?

_____

_____

2. Have you ever lost control of something, even though you thought you wouldn't?

_____

_____

Prayer

God, please help me to have control over what I do and say so that I don't hurt others or myself. Amen.

BOTTLE BUBBLES

Read this to your child: "It's important to have control. God wants you to control what you do so you don't hurt yourself or others. Here's a way to control the air inside a bottle."

What You Need

plastic soda bottle

water

What to Do

1. Hold your thumb over the opening of the soda bottle.

2. Push the entire bottle underwater (a kitchen sink or bathtub works well for this).

3. You'll see that you control the air in the bottle. You can leave the air inside the bottle or let it out to bubble to the surface.

CHOICES

Being good is a matter of choice.
Make the most of every opportunity.

– Colossians 4:5

José's Choice

It was a lovely day to honor Grandma's birthday, and the whole family went to a chicken barbecue to celebrate. As José sat down at the long table next to his Aunt Theresa, she leaned over and whispered in his ear, "Now remember, you're sitting next to me, so no throwing food or making a big mess."

"I never throw my food," said José with a little giggle. He knew that Aunt Theresa didn't allow messy eating and he didn't want her to be upset with him. He was always extra careful when he was with her, even though he was a very messy eater at home.

When the meal was over, José's mommy said, "My, how nice you ate!"

Aunt Theresa pointed out that José was able to eat neatly when he tried. José was very proud of himself.

José ate neatly when he was with Aunt Theresa because he chose to do so. When he was at home, he wanted to be messy and didn't care if that was a bad way to act.

Being good is always a choice. God wants you to always choose to be good.

Your Turn

1. Can you remember a time when you chose to be bad instead of good?

_____

_____

2. When is it difficult to be good?

_____

_____

Prayer

God, please help me to remember that being good is a choice that I make. Help me to always make the right choices. Amen.

CHOICES TO MAKE

Read this to your child: "Being good is a choice you make. God wants you to always choose to be good and live your life as He wants. Here are some situations that involve making a choice. Draw a line from the situation on the top to the choice you would make below it."

 USES

Most things have more than one use.

He who works his land will have abundant food.
– Proverbs 12:11

In Mommy's Honor

"I made it in honor of you, Mommy," Nathan said as he showed her his latest creation. He and his sister Emma had arranged play food on the living room floor so that it would look like a bird.

"How is this in honor of me?" Mommy asked.

"It's because you like birds so much," Nathan explained.

"That's wonderful," said Mommy. "It was so creative of you to think of making your play food look like something else. I'm so proud of you," Mommy said as she gave Nathan a big hug.

Nathan found two uses for his toys. First, he was creative with his toys. Second, he did something special for his mommy with his toys. God made many things for you. Find as many uses as you can for His creation.

Your Turn

1. Why did Nathan make his play food look like a bird?

_____

_____

2. Have you ever used a toy in more than one way?

_____

_____

Prayer

God, thank You for all Your wonderful gifts that I can use in many different ways. Amen.

FOOD FRIENDS

Read this to your child: "God wants you to make the most of all His gifts, and that means sometimes using things as many ways as you can. Here's how Nathan made his toy food bird. Maybe you can make things with your toys as well. Ask Mommy or Daddy to take a picture of what you make with your toys when you're done. You can finish coloring this picture of Nathan's toys."

COMPROMISE

God wants me to get along with others.

*You are...fellow citizens with God's people
and members of God's household.*

– Ephesians 2:19

Logan's Nest

Logan liked to sleep with Mommy and Daddy. They didn't mind Logan sleeping with them from time to time, but their bed just wasn't big enough for three people. They tried to squeeze him in at night, but Logan just wouldn't stay put. Each night he would roll and roll and Mommy and Daddy would be awakened over and over.

After many nights of this, Mommy had an idea. She decided she would let Logan make a little bed on the floor next to their bed. That way, Logan could be with them, but he wouldn't bother them at night.

Logan thought this was a fine idea. He carefully laid out blankets, his sleeping bag and even Mommy and Daddy's comforter from their bed.

Then Logan stood over his new sleeping spot and said, "This is my nest!"

Mommy and Daddy found a way to compromise with Logan. That means that they took a little of what he wanted, and a little of what they wanted, and put them together. That way, they were all happy. God likes when people do their best to get along and be happy. Sometimes, that means you have to compromise.

Your Turn

1. Can you think of another way that Logan could have compromised with his Mommy and Daddy?

_____

_____

2. Tell about a time you compromised.

_____

_____

Prayer

Dear God, help me to remember that I don't always have to have everything I want. Sometimes it's okay to compromise. Amen.

FINDING COMPROMISE

Read this to your child: "God wants everyone to get along, so sometimes it's okay to compromise. Look at the pictures below and match each one to what would be a good compromise."

MEASUREMENTS

God measures by what's on the inside.

*Man looks at the outward appearance,
but the Lord looks at the heart.*

– 1 Samuel 16:7

How Tall Am I?

Kevin stood on the scale and looked down at the numbers.

"How tall am I?" he called to Daddy.

"That doesn't tell you how tall you are," said Daddy. "It tells you how heavy you are…you know, how much you weigh."

The next week, Kevin stood on the scale and asked again, "How tall am I, Daddy?"

Daddy once again explained that the scale measured weight, not height. But no matter how many times Daddy and Kevin talked about the scale, Kevin always went to it thinking it would tell him his height. He thought height was the only important way to measure someone. It was the only way he wanted to be measured.

There are many ways to measure someone. You can measure height and weight, but you can also measure people by how nice they are, how they love God and if they keep their promises. Who you are inside is much more important than your physical height or weight. God measures you by who you are on the inside.

Your Turn

1. What are some ways that you can measure people?

_____

_____

2. How does God measure people?

_____

_____

Prayer

Thank You, God, for only measuring me by who I am on the inside. Amen.

MEASURING

Read this to your child: "God wants you to measure people by who they are on the inside, not what they look like. Here are some things to measure. Ask Mommy or Daddy to help you use a tape measurer or ruler to measure each one."

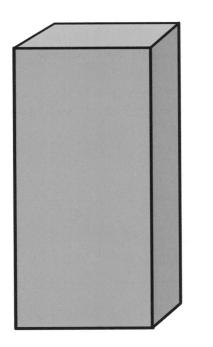

MANNERS

I should have good manners.

Each of you should look...to the interests of others.
– Philippians 2:4

Do Only Germans Have Good Manners?

Julian was Gabriel's best friend. They had been friends since Julian and his family had moved from Germany to Gabriel's town.

One day, Julian came to Gabriel's house for a visit. Gabriel's mom made a special treat: cake with lots of vanilla icing and red sprinkles.

Julian and Gabriel each had a large slice of cake and a cold glass of milk. After he was finished eating, Julian carefully carried his plate and glass from the table and set them in the sink. Gabriel watched from his seat.

"Gabriel, I want you to look at Julian," said Mommy. "See how polite he is? He didn't make a mess at the table, and he cleared his plate when he was done."

"That must be because he's German" said Gabriel.

"That doesn't matter," said Julian. "It doesn't matter who you are. Everyone should have good manners."

Julian was right. It doesn't matter who you are or where you are. God wants you to be kind to everyone, and that means having good manners.

Your Turn

1. Name some ways to show good manners.

_____

_____

2. Do you always have good manners?

_____

_____

Prayer

God, please help me to remember to have good manners all the time. Amen.

MANNERS MATTER

Read this to your child: "God wants you to have good manners all the time because He wants you to treat everyone well. Here are some situations that call for good manners. Look at each picture and then talk with your mommy or daddy about how the boy in each picture could show good manners or bad manners."

PERMISSION

I should ask myself what Jesus would do.

Turn from evil and do good.

– Psalm 37:27

Kaylee's Bus Ride

Caleb wanted his friend Kaylee to come over to play after school, but he didn't have permission from his mom. When it came time to go home, Caleb told Kaylee to get on the bus with him anyway.

But when the bus got to Caleb's stop, the bus driver wouldn't let Kaylee get off. He said that because it wasn't her house, she needed to have permission to leave at that stop.

The bus driver had to use his special radio to call Caleb's mom. Meanwhile, the other kids had to wait. They were going to be late to their stops because the driver was busy calling Caleb's mom and couldn't drive.

After Caleb's mom said it was okay, the driver finally let Kaylee get off the bus at Caleb's stop. Kaylee and Caleb were both embarrassed, but they had learned a lesson. Now they understood that they should always ask permission first before doing something.

It is important to follow the rules and get permission first. That way, you find out from a grown-up if you are doing the right thing. In the same way, when you are unsure about a choice, you should ask yourself what Jesus would do. Jesus always knows how to do the right thing.

Your Turn

1. Why should you always get permission before doing something?

_____

_____

2. What should you do when you are unsure about a choice?

_____

_____

Prayer

God, help me to remember that I should get permission from Mommy or Daddy before doing things. Amen.

REMEMBER BRACELET

Read this to your child: "Everyone needs permission from someone–even your mommy and daddy. They need to have permission from Jesus for everything they do. That's why before doing something, you should ask yourself what Jesus would want you to do first. If you make the bracelet below, it could help you to remember to do only what Jesus would want you to do."

What You Need

ribbon

macaroni

buttons

straws

What to Do

1. There are many ways you can do this. The only limit is your imagination. Try braiding different colors of ribbon together and then stringing macaroni through them, alternating with pieces of striped straws. You could also use buttons, or anything else that you have around the house.

2. The first step should be to measure the child's wrist. Remember to allow for enough length so the bracelet can easily slip over the child's hand but is not so loose that it falls off.

3. Use that measurement to cut a piece of ribbon and tie a knot at the end.

4. As you place each item on your bracelet, think about how God loves and cares for you and wants you to love and care for others. The bracelet should remind you to behave as God wants as you go through your day.

5. After you string the items on the ribbon, simply tie the two ends together.

Note: If you want to make a necklace, you should use breakable elastic instead of ribbon, for safety.

RIGIDITY

I can trust God to plan my life.

Do not store up for yourselves treasures on earth...
store up for yourselves treasures in heaven.
– Matthew 6:19-20

Perfect Pizza

Tommy was so happy! His mommy and daddy said they would pick up a pizza that he could eat in the car while they were driving. They had even ordered one of his favorite kinds: pepperoni and pineapple.

"Uh-oh," Mommy said as they drove away from the pizza parlor. "They messed up the order. This pizza has bacon and black olives on it instead of pepperoni and pineapple."

"Take it back!" yelled Tommy, "It's wrong, so they should take it back."

"We don't have time to take it back," said Mommy. "Black olive and bacon is one of your favorite kinds, too, so this will be fine."

"Take it back. It's wrong!" hollered Tommy.

"You're right, honey," said Mommy, "but sometimes you just have to let things go. We're in a big hurry today, so we can't wait for a new pizza."

Tommy knew they were in a hurry, but he didn't care. He refused to eat the pizza, so his sisters ate it. Tommy pouted and missed dinner.

Sometimes things don't work out exactly the way you want. You can plan your life, but only God is really in charge of what happens. He has a special plan for your life. When things don't go your way, trust that God knows what is happening.

Your Turn

1. Tell about a time you had to do something that wasn't what you planned.

_____

_____

2. Who is in charge of your life?

_____

_____

Prayer

God, please help me to remember that You are in charge of my life. I know You have a special plan for me. Amen.

PICKY PIZZA

Read this to your child: "Tommy decided that if he couldn't have exactly what he wanted, then he would have nothing. But even though your plans don't work out sometimes, you can trust that God has a special plan for your life. Here's a pizza you can plan. Draw the toppings you like on your pizza."

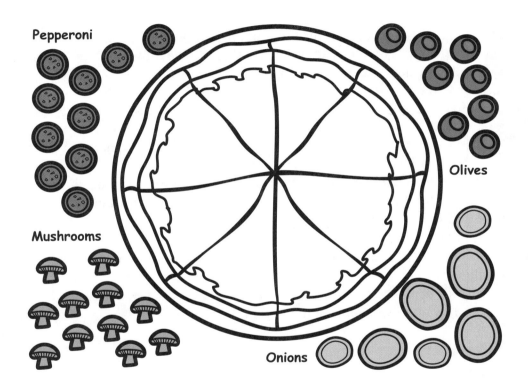

HAPPINESS

God wants me to share my happiness.

Come and share your...happiness!

– Matthew 25:21

Jason's Penguins

"Can I call Grandpa?" Jason asked as he came through the front door.

Jason's whole family had just come home from visiting the children's zoo. He had waited all year for the penguin exhibit, and when he finally saw it, a feeling of wonderful warmth and joy flowed through him. Jason was so happy about seeing the penguins that he just had to call and tell Grandpa all about it.

"Here you go," Mommy said as she dialed Grandpa's phone number and handed Jason the receiver.

"Grandpa, Grandpa," Jason yelled when he heard his grandpa's voice, "you'll never believe what I saw today!"

Jason talked and talked. He was so happy about the penguins that soon Grandpa was feeling happy, too. He told Jason about when he was little and went to the zoo, and the animals he was happy to see. Jason and Grandpa were happy together.

Jason was so happy about the penguins that he wanted to share his happiness with his grandpa. That's wonderful. God wants for you to share your happiness with others. If they see how happy you are, maybe they will want to welcome God into their lives, too!

Your Turn

1. Can you think of something that makes you happy, and that you'd like to share?

_____

_____

2. Why does God want you to share your happiness?

_____

_____

Prayer

God, thank You for giving me so many happy things to share. Amen.

MATCHING ANIMALS

Read this to your child: "God wants you to share your happiness. Jason shared his happiness about the zoo. Look at the zoo animals below. Circle the one in each row that is different."

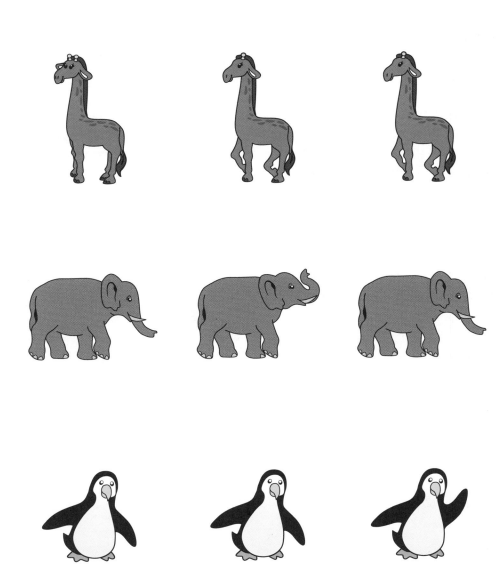

BRAGGING

It does not honor God to brag.

Do nothing out of...vain conceit.

– Philippians 2:3

Zane's Game

Jordan was excited to be going to Zane's house just after Christmas. He was looking forward to seeing Zane's Christmas presents and playing with his new computer games.

As they rode to Zane's house, Jordan laughed at Zane's description of how he and his sisters made up their own chasing game to play in the basement that week. Zane talked and talked about how the game was played, but Jordan knew what Zane would say when it came time to tell who won the game.

"My sisters were winning for a while...," Zane began.

"But you won, right?" interrupted Jordan, knowing that Zane was going to say he won. Zane always liked to brag when he won at something.

God wants you to be proud of yourself, but you shouldn't brag. Bragging can hurt others' feelings. If you win or lose, just have fun doing it. If you are good at something, try to get even better. But whatever you do, don't brag about it.

Your Turn

1. Do you ever brag about something you've done?

_____

_____

2. What can you do instead of bragging?

_____

_____

Prayer

God, please help me to be proud of what I can do, but not to brag about it. Amen.

HUMBLING CREATION

Read this to your child: "God doesn't want you to brag like Zane always did. God is much bigger than anything we can do. One way to remember that is by looking at the wonderful world God made. Ask Mommy or Daddy to help you with this activity, and you'll see some of God's tiniest creations come to life."

What You Need

clear container

brine shrimp eggs
(available at most pet stores)

kosher salt

dry yeast

measuring spoon

What to Do

1. Fill your container with water and allow it to sit for 24 hours, as you would for an   aquarium.

2. Add about one tablespoon of salt per liter of water, and stir it up.

3. Sprinkle the brine shrimp on top of the water.

4. In a few days, the shrimp will hatch.

5. Sprinkle a tiny amount of yeast on the water every two to three days to feed the shrimp.

STEWARDSHIP

God wants me to care for His world.

*Then God said, "Let us make man in our image...
and let them rule over...all the earth."*
– Genesis 1:26

For the Birds

"Time to feed the birds," said Mommy.

"Yea!" yelled Billy. He loved feeding the birds, especially in the winter when Mommy would let him help with the special bagel feeders they made for the birds.

Mommy placed a jar of peanut butter, a butter knife and a bagel on a paper towel. Billy happily spread the peanut butter on the bagel, then rolled it in birdseed.

"Mine's going to be big and juicy," Billy said as he worked.

When he was almost done, Mommy hung the bagel by the window where they could watch the birds come to eat. The hungry birds soon were peeping and eating happily.

God wants us to care for His world. Billy fed the birds in the winter because that's a time when they can use extra help finding food. Billy was being a good steward of God's creation by helping to feed the birds.

Your Turn

1. Why did Billy feed the birds in the winter?

_____

_____

2. What do you do to be a good steward of God's creation?

_____

_____

Prayer

Help me, God, to be a good steward of Your creation. Amen.

PEANUT BUTTER FEEDER

Read this to your child: "God made a beautiful world for you, and He expects you to help take good care of it. One way to do that is to feed the birds in the winter when they need a little extra help finding food. You can make the same special bagel feeder that Billy made by following the directions below."

What You Need

bagel

peanut butter (chunky is best)

butter knife

birdseed

twine or string

What to Do

1. Tie a piece of twine around the middle of the bagel.

2. Use a butter knife to spread the peanut butter. If you warm the peanut butter for just a few seconds in the microwave, it will spread easier. But be careful not to warm it too much because it won't stick as well if it's runny.

3. Be sure to slather on plenty of peanut butter.

4. When you're done, roll the bagel in birdseed. Roll it several times so it picks up as much seed as possible.

5. Hang the feeder outside and watch the birds enjoy their special treat.

I should act with good sense.

The discerning heart seeks knowledge.

– Proverbs 15:14

Bedroom Bugs

Cameron liked bugs. He liked to go for long nature walks and look close-up at bugs. He would hold bugs in his hand, and even let them walk on his clothes. Sometimes he would put them in a "bug box" so he could feed them, and keep them for a long time.

As much as Cameron liked bugs, however, he did not like them when they were in his room. He wouldn't go near a bug if it was in his room. When Cameron would find a bug in his bedroom, he would run away, yelling and screaming. Mommy always had to come and get the bug for him. Sometimes Cameron would get so scared of a bug in his room that he would cry, even though he never cried when he played with bugs outside.

Cameron's fear of bugs only when they were in his room didn't make any sense. The bugs in his room weren't any different from the bugs Cameron played with outside, yet he acted very differently with them. That didn't make sense! Before you act, think about what makes sense. Ask God to help you to know what makes sense.

Your Turn

1. Is there something that doesn't make sense in your life?

_____

_____

2. Who can you ask to help you know what makes sense?

_____

_____

Prayer

God, please help me to act with good sense. Amen.

BUG BOX

Read this to your child: "God wants you to act with good sense and think things through clearly. If you follow the directions below, your 'bug box' will make sense–it will work!"

What You Need

a shoe box

clear plastic wrap

foil

tape

scissors

crayons

dirt, grass or wood chips

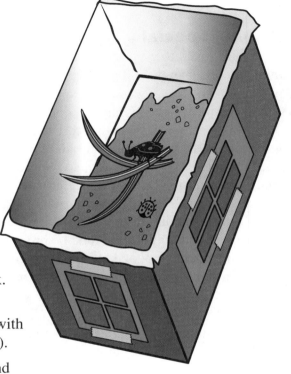

What to Do

1. Cut square holes in the top and sides of a shoe box.

2. Cover the holes with clear plastic wrap and secure it with tape (these act as windows).

3. Form foil to the bottom, and partway up the sides of the inside of the box (you can also use plastic wrap, but it doesn't stay in place as well).

4. Fill the box with a thin layer of dirt, grass or wood chips.

5. Decorate your box with crayons. Now you're ready to gather some bugs!

Note: The nice thing about this bug box is that it can simply be thrown out when it gets dirty and can be easily replaced.

SPECIAL

God wants me to feel special.

The Spirit of God lives in you.

– Romans 8:9

Feeling Special

Victor loved to go places with Grandma. It was one of his favorite things to do. They would go shopping and sometimes even eat at a fancy restaurant–and today was a day to do just that.

As Victor watched Grandma doing some shopping, he noticed that there was a person outside the store at a booth. The person at the booth was painting little drawings on kids' faces. It looked like a lot of fun! Victor wanted to have fun, too, so he asked Grandma to take him for some face painting. The face painter used a tiny brush to carefully draw Victor's favorite cartoon character on his cheek. Victor felt so special!

When Grandma took Victor to the restaurant, she noticed that he was eating in an odd way. Every time he brought a spoonful of food up to his mouth, he would stop, open his mouth very wide, and then carefully put the spoon in his mouth. Usually, Victor was a fast and messy eater, so Grandma wondered why he was eating so slowly and neatly.

As time passed, Grandma finally realized what was going on. Victor didn't want to get food on his face and cover his face paint!

Sometimes the tiniest things can make you feel extra special. God likes that. He wants you to feel how special you are every day, and not just because of things you have, but by remembering how much He loves you.

Your Turn

1. What made Victor feel special?

_____

_____

2. What makes you feel special?

_____

_____

Prayer

God, please help me to remember how special I am. Amen.

SPECIAL THINGS

Read this to your child: "God wants you to feel special all the time, because He loves you so much. Below are some pictures of special things for you to finish coloring."

EMPATHY

I should try to understand the feelings of others.

Let us encourage one another.

– Hebrews 10:25

Brat

Kyle liked his new friend Bret. He told his mommy and daddy all about Bret and how he was invited to Bret's house, but every time he said Bret's name, he said "Brat" instead.

"Why do you call him 'Brat'?" asked Daddy. "Does he act naughty?"

"No," answered Kyle. "He's really nice."

"Then why do you call him 'Brat'?" Daddy asked again.

"That's just the way I say it," said Kyle with a snicker.

Daddy tried to get Kyle to say Bret's name correctly because he thought Bret might feel bad about being called "Brat," but Kyle just kept saying "Brat" anyway.

Kyle didn't want to say Bret's name correctly. He didn't care that saying his name wrong could hurt Bret's feelings. Kyle didn't understand how Bret would feel, and so he didn't care. God wouldn't have liked what Kyle did. God wants you to always try to understand how other people feel, and do your best not to hurt others. God wants you to show empathy.

Your Turn

1. Have you ever done something mean even when you knew itwamean?

_____

_____

2. What would God have wanted you to do in that situation?

_____

_____

Prayer

God, please help me to remember other people's feelings so that I don't do things to hurt them. Amen.

DIFFERENCES

Read this to your child: "God wants you to think about how other people feel, and be careful not to do anything that would hurt them. In the story, the words 'Bret' and 'Brat' sounded alike. Below are some pictures of butterflies that look alike, but one is different. Can you find it?"

CLEANLINESS

I should keep my body clean.

I am clean and without sin.

– Proverbs 20:9

Jason's Bath

Whenever Mommy told Jason it was time to take a bath, he said, "I can't take a bath."

Jason hated baths. He hated everything about baths. He thought the water was too wet, the soap was too slimy and the washcloth was scratchy. And he disliked that when he was wet he felt cold and shivery.

Mommy waited as long as she could before telling Jason he had to take a bath. But no matter how long it had been, or how dirty Jason was, he still ran away, yelling, "I can't take a bath!"

When Mommy finally caught Jason, he screamed, "I can't take a bath!" over and over again. He kept screaming while Mommy was washing him. He didn't care that baths made him clean. Jason hated baths.

God wouldn't have liked how Jason behaved. God wants you to do what your mommy tells you to do, because she knows what's best. God also wants you to take good care of the body He has given you. That means staying clean. If you don't stay clean, your body could become sick. God wants you to stay clean and healthy.

Your Turn

1. Why is it important to keep your body clean?

_____

_____

2. Is there something that you hate to do?

_____

_____

Prayer

God, thank You for giving me a wonderful body. Please help me to remember that it's important to keep myself clean. Amen.

KEEPING CLEAN

Read this to your child: "God gave you a wonderful body so you should take good care of it. That means washing yourself when you get dirty. Look at the picture below and circle all the things that can be used to keep you clean."

INSECURITY

Parents (and God) never run out of love.

The eternal God is your refuge.

– Deuteronomy 33:27

Enough Love

"Stop it, Jack," yelled Luke as he pushed him away from Mommy.

"But I want to snuggle with Mommy," Jack yelled back. "You go away!"

Luke and Jack pushed and pulled at each other as they both tried to attach themselves to Mommy's legs. They each wanted to be the one to snuggle with Mommy, and Luke was getting so upset that he started to cry.

"Mommy," Luke cried, "Jack's making you not love me!"

Luke was worried that if Mommy spent more time with Jack, she would love Luke less. He didn't understand that parents can love more than one child at the same time. Love doesn't run out, so parents always have plenty of love for their children.

God's love is like a parent's love. God will always love you, no matter how many other people He loves, too. You don't ever have to worry that God will run out of love for you.

Your Turn

1. Do you ever worry that Mommy or Daddy won't have enough love for you?

_____

_____

2. Who loves you even more than Mommy or Daddy?

_____

_____

Prayer

God, please help me to remember that Your love will always be there for me. Amen.

PAPER BAG PIÑATA

Read this to your child: "God's love never runs out. He has enough love for everyone. Here's something you can make to enjoy with your family and friends. It won't run out of loving treats and surprises until there's enough for everyone."

What You Need

paper grocery bag

paper streamers

crayons

string or twine

candy and small toys

What to Do

1. Decorate a paper bag with crayons.

2. Poke a hole on each side of the bottom of the paper bag.

3. Thread a piece of string through each hole (this is what you will hang the piñata from–it hangs upside down).

4. Fill the bag with candy and toys (half-full is best).

5. Fold over the opening of the piñata and staple it a few times, attaching a colorful streamer with each staple.

6. Hang the piñata.

7. With sticks, wooden spoons or plastic bats, have each blindfolded person take a turn whacking at the piñata until it breaks and the treats spill out.

WORTH

God's love is worth more than anything.

The world and its desires pass away,
but the...will of God lives forever.

– 1 John 2:17

Snow Diamonds

It had finally snowed! Connor had waited and waited for the winter snow to come. When it finally did, he couldn't wait to get outside and play.

As Connor hopped through the drifts around his house, he noticed that there were some shiny icy spots in the snow. They were some of the most beautiful things Connor had ever seen, so he named them "snow diamonds."

Connor remembered his Mommy's pretty sparkling rings, and that she had told him they were worth a lot of money. He knew, just looking at his shiny snow diamonds, that they must also be worth a great deal. So Connor gathered up as many snow diamonds as he could and put them in a special hole he dug in the snow just to store his treasures. When the snow melted, so did Connor's diamonds, but while it was still cold, he had them to enjoy.

Connor's snow diamonds were worth just as much to him as real diamonds, because to him they were just as beautiful and precious. He knew that what something is worth isn't decided by how much money it costs. In the same way, God's love for you isn't decided by how you act, or what you think. God's love is worth a great deal, even though it's free.

Your Turn

1. Can you think of something that doesn't cost anything, but is worth a lot to you anyway?

_____

_____

2. How much is God's love worth?

_____

_____

Prayer

Thank You, God, for giving me Your love for free. Amen.

WHICH IS WORTH MORE?

Read this to your child: "God's love is free, yet it's worth more than anything else in the world. Look at the things below. Which one is worth the most? Circle it."

STEALING

Stealing is wrong.

He must return what he has stolen.

– Leviticus 6:4

Playing Indians

Luis and his brother, Isaac, loved to watch their big sister, Kendall, put on makeup. They knew that they could only watch. They were not allowed to play with Kendall's makeup.

One day when Kendall was at school, Luis and Isaac sneaked a peek into Kendall's makeup drawer in the bathroom. They liked all the pretty colors.

Luis and Isaac thought the makeup would make great Indian war paint, so they just couldn't resist painting it on their faces. And then onto the bathroom counter. And then in the sink. And then all over the mirror. To them, it looked like a beautiful work of art!

When Luis and Isaac looked in the mirror, they decided they had done a very good job with their Indian war paint. So they ran to show Mommy. But Mommy didn't like what she saw.

Luis and Isaac did two bad things. They stole their sister's makeup, and then they used it to make a big mess in the bathroom. God wouldn't like that. In the Bible, God says, "Do not steal." It makes God sad when you do bad things. Make God happy by always trying to do what is right.

Your Turn

1. Have you ever stolen anything?

_____

_____

2. Why is stealing wrong?

_____

_____

Prayer

God, please help me to remember that I should never steal anything. Amen.

RIBBON CHIMES

Read this to your child: "Stealing is a bad thing to do. God wants you only to do good things. Here's a good thing to do that will make pretty music for your whole family."

What You Need

ribbon

metal ring from canning jar

miscellaneous metal items (see below)

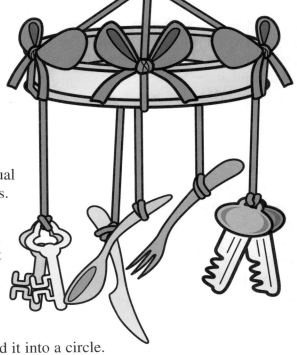

What to Do

1. Cut a ribbon into four equal lengths of about 12 inches.

2. Attach the ribbon at four points, at equal distances, on your ring. If you don't have a canning jar ring, any sturdy, but light, ring-shaped object will do. You can even use a wire coat hanger and bend it into a circle.

3. Gather the loose ends of the four ribbons together and tie a knot (the ring will hang from this).

4. To the bottom of the ring, tie more ribbons (at varying lengths so your "chimes" won't tangle). You can now tie your metal items to each of these hanging ribbons.

5. Hang your chimes in the wind and enjoy!

Metal item ideas: canning jar rings, soda can tabs, refrigerated dough tube ends, old silverware, measuring cups, etc.

DEPENDENCY

I can depend on God.

His love endures forever.

– 2 Chronicles 20:21

Boo-Boo Thumb

"Try to not suck my thumb. Try to not suck my thumb," said Brian over and over again as he lay snuggled in his Mommy's arms. He had a small cut at the bottom of his sucking thumb, and he didn't want to suck on it until it was all better.

"I can't fall asleep if I don't suck my thumb," Brian cried.

"Don't worry," said Mommy, "I'll hold your hand, and before you know it, you'll be fast asleep."

"But I can't fall asleep if I don't suck my thumb," Brian whined again.

Brian squirmed and wiggled. Several times his hand tried to creep up to his mouth, but Mommy held his hand firm so he couldn't pop his thumb in. Soon, he settled into a sound sleep.

Brian learned that he didn't need to suck his thumb in order to fall asleep. Sometimes the things on which you depend aren't really as important as you think they are. The only thing you should always depend on is God. His love and care is dependable!

Your Turn

1. Why did Brian want to suck his thumb?

_____

_____

2. Who is always dependable?

_____

_____

Prayer

Dear God, thank You for always being dependable. I know I can count on Your love and care. Amen.

PENCIL ORNAMENT

Read this to your child: "You can always depend on God for what's important. But we depend on many other, less important things, too, such as flipping a switch to turn on lights in a room. For what do you depend on a pencil? Here's something to decorate your favorite pencil."

What You Need

pencil

empty thread spool

glue

glitter

crayons

ribbons

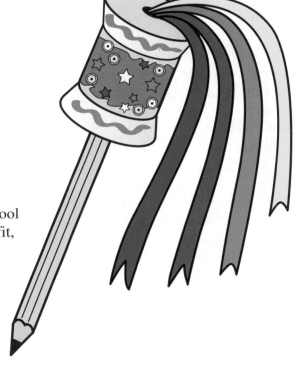

What to Do

1. Fit an empty thread spool to a pencil (most will fit, but make sure first).

2. Spread glue on the spool, then roll it in glitter (if you don't like glitter, you can just color the spool with crayons).

3. Glue ribbons on one end of the spool.

4. After the spool is dry, stick it on the end of your pencil.

TEASING

God wants me to have fun as long as no one gets hurt.

The wise in heart are called discerning.

– Proverbs 16:21

Eating Eyeballs

"How can you do it?" Daddy asked Juan. "How can you eat that sandwich with it staring right back at you?"

Daddy had made Juan's butter sandwich just the way he liked it, with two green olives stuck in the top of it with toothpicks. The red pimentos in the centers of the olives made them look like eyes.

Juan grinned as he slowly brought the sandwich closer to his mouth and took a big bite. Then he popped one of the olives into his mouth.

"Oh no!" cried Daddy, laughing. "You ate his eyeball!"

"It's not an eyeball," laughed Juan. "It's not real!" He pulled the other olive off and ate it, too.

"Not another one!" pretended Daddy, covering his eyes. Juan laughed.

Teasing is okay when it doesn't hurt anyone. Juan and Daddy teased each other about eating "eyeballs," but they knew those eyeballs were really olives. Juan knew Daddy was having just as much fun as Juan was with his teasing. It's all right to tease as long as everyone is in on the joke. God wants you to have fun as long as no one gets hurt.

Your Turn

1. Why did Juan and Daddy call the olives "eyeballs"?

_____

_____

2. When was the last time you teased someone? Did you do it in a good way, or a bad way?

_____

_____

Prayer

God, please help me to remember that it's only okay to tease people if it's done in a good way. Amen.

OLIVE EYEBALLS

Read this to your child: "God wants you to have fun, and sometimes that involves teasing other people. But teasing is only okay if everyone is having fun. Juan and his daddy had fun teasing because of the sandwich he made for him. Here's how Juan's daddy made Juan's sandwich. You and your daddy can make a sandwich just like it!"

What You Need

bread

butter (or whatever filling you like)

green olives with pimento centers

toothpicks

What to Do

1. Spread the filling on one slice of bread.

2. Lightly fold over the slice so it flops open a bit, and looks more like a mouth.

3. Skewer two olives, one per toothpick.

4. Stick the toothpicks in the top of the sandwich with the pimento side of the olive facing the open part of the sandwich.

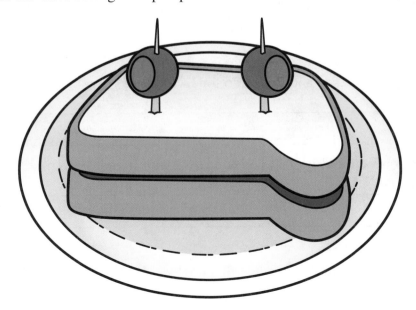

COOPERATION

God wants me to cooperate.

Agree with one another so that there may be no divisions among you.

– 1 Corinthians 1:10

Combing Rats

Jackson and Becky loved to play together. They were only one year apart, so they liked a lot of the same things.

Becky had long, blond hair that needed a lot of brushing to keep it smooth. Even though Jackson's hair was shorter, his hair would still tangle sometimes, too.

Mommy had once said Becky's hair was "ratty," so Jackson liked to call the tangles in their hair "rats." These hair rats were very hard to get out.

One day as they were playing, Jackson decided to help Becky with her hair. Using his fingers as a comb, he carefully pulled his fingers through Becky's hair, removing several rats as he did.

When he was done, it was Becky's turn to get out Jackson's rats. Jackson noticed that when Becky combed out his rats it didn't hurt as much as when Mommy did it. With Becky, it was actually fun! Jackson and Becky agreed that they would always comb out each other's rats.

Jackson and Becky worked together to get their "rats" out. They cooperated. God likes when you cooperate with other people. When you cooperate, life is better for everyone.

Your Turn

1. What did Jackson and Becky do for each other?

_____

_____

2. What are some ways that you cooperate with friends or family?

_____

_____

Prayer

God, please help me to remember that it is good to cooperate with others. Amen.

STAINED-WAX WINDOWS

Read this to your child: "God likes when you cooperate with others. If you cooperate with an adult for this project, you'll have a pretty stained glass picture to put in your window."

What You Need

wax paper

rags

iron

crayons

grater or sharp knife

What to Do

1. Use a grater (or sharp knife) to make crayon shavings.

2. Sprinkle the shavings between two pieces of wax paper.

3. Set the paper on top of a rag.

4. Place another rag on top of the wax paper.

5. Use a warm iron to melt the crayons into the paper.

6. Allow to cool, then place the picture in a window to enjoy.

Note: For more of a stained glass effect, use very fine shavings and spread them out evenly. If the shavings are too thick, they will simply be blobs of color.

SHAME

I can make a mistake without feeling shameful.

May he work in us what is pleasing to him.
– Hebrews 13:21

Eric's Shame

Eric loved to be tucked in bed between Mommy and Daddy. It was such a warm and snuggly feeling!

Eric, Mommy and Daddy all slept safe and sound until suddenly Eric had a bad dream and started to whip his arms around. One of his hands hit Mommy right in the eye! Then Eric started to kick. He kicked Mommy so hard that he almost pushed her over the edge of the bed!

When morning came and Eric heard what he had done, he felt very bad. He felt ashamed.

Eric learned that when he was asleep he did some things that he didn't mean to do. Life is like that. You don't always have control over everything you do. Sometimes you might do things you don't mean to do, such as wet the bed or break a toy. There is no reason to feel shame for what you do by accident. God understands we all make mistakes.

Your Turn

1. Have you felt shameful for doing something that simply was a mistake?

_____

_____

2. What can you do to feel better when you make a mistake?

_____

_____

Prayer

God, please help me not to make mistakes. But I know making mistakes is part of learning and not something shameful. Amen.

ASHAMED, OR NOT?

Read this to your child: "God doesn't want you to be ashamed of making mistakes. Look at the pictures below. Draw a circle around the boy doing things that are honest mistakes and not shameful. Draw an X through the pictures where the boy is behaving badly on purpose."

EXPECTATIONS

I can expect God always to love and care for me.

God has said, "Never will I leave you."

– Hebrews 13:5

Mason's Expectations

"I love you, Evan," said Mommy as he got out of the van.

"I love you, Alexis," said Mommy to Alexis as she followed Evan out.

Mason was next. Mommy called after him, "I love you, Mason. And don't walk into the wrong classroom." Once Evan had seen Mason walk into a different class, so Mommy liked to tease Mason about it.

"Oh, Mom," Mason giggled as he hauled out his back-pack.

Mommy and baby Vanessa waved goodbye to the kids as the van pulled away. This was their normal morning routine.

The next day, Mommy was busy doing laundry in the basement, so Daddy took the kids to school.

When Mason got home from school and saw Mommy, he had tears in his eyes. Mommy asked him what was wrong. Mason asked, "Why didn't you say the things you always say when we leave?"

Mommy hadn't realized how important the routine was to Mason. Even though Mommy teased him each morning, hearing the same words each day made him feel loved and secure. He expected it. In the same way, your expectations of God's love and guidance are important. But God never gets too busy to be who you expect Him to be.

Your Turn

1. Can you think of some expectations you have of your mommy or daddy?

_____

_____

2. What are some expectations you have of God?

_____

_____

Prayer

God, thank You for always being as wonderful as I expect You to be. Amen.

SOUND EXPECTATIONS

Read this to your child: "You can always expect a lot from God. He will never be too busy to love and care for you. Here's something you can expect to be a lot of fun. Have Mommy or Daddy fill soda bottles with water, each at a different level. Now blow air across the top. Notice that the sound you make with each bottle is different depending upon the amount of water in them."

INCONSIDERATE

God wants me to be considerate of others.

Love your neighbor as yourself.

– James 2:8

Carlos's Rolls

"Please don't eat any more rolls," said Mommy to Miguel. "The rest of those are for Carlos."

"Okay," said Miguel as he ate his second cinnamon roll. But when Mommy left the kitchen, Miguel quickly grabbed the last two rolls.

"Mmmm," he said as he licked off the sweet icing.

But just as Miguel was chewing his last bite, Carlos came into the kitchen.

"Mom!" he yelled. "Miguel ate my rolls!"

Mommy came into the kitchen to see Carlos with tears in his eyes and Miguel acting like he had done nothing wrong. The plate was empty.

Mommy punished Miguel for not following directions. The next time she made cinnamon rolls, Miguel had to give his share to Carlos. Miguel didn't get any rolls at all.

It was naughty of Miguel to eat Carlos's rolls, especially after saying that he wouldn't. He was inconsiderate of Carlos's feelings, which means he didn't care about how Carlos would feel.

The Bible says to treat others as you would like to be treated. God doesn't want you to be inconsiderate of others.

Your Turn

1. How did Miguel know that he wasn't supposed to eat the rolls?

_____

_____

2. Have you ever done something without thinking about how it would make the other person feel?

_____

_____

Prayer

God, please help me to remember that I should be considerate of others. I should think about how they feel, not just about my own feelings. Amen.

JUICE CUBES

Read this to your child: "God wants you to be considerate of others. Miguel had to give his rolls to Carlos to make up for what he did. Here's a special treat you can make. Be considerate as you give each of your friends or family a juice cube."

What You Need

ice cube tray

juice

toothpicks

plastic wrap

What to Do

1. Fill an ice cube tray with any kind of juice.

2. Cover the tray with plastic wrap.

3. Poke a toothpick through the wrap and into each cube (the wrap keeps the toothpick upright).

4. Place the tray in the freezer.

5. When the cubes are frozen solid, remove the wrap and enjoy!

ATTENTION

I need to pay attention to lessons about God and the Bible.

Listen, my son, and be wise.

– Proverbs 23:19

Simon's Sewer Water

Simon was excited–and a little afraid–as he watched the big truck lower the long metal pole into the ground. Daddy said the man was drilling a well so that they could have water, but Simon didn't understand.

"We already have water," Simon said. "We have sewer water."

"It's not 'sewer' water," Daddy corrected. "We have a 'cistern,' which is a big box that holds water. But it's not enough for us so we're drilling deep into the ground to get water from there, too."

Daddy also explained that sewer water is bad, yucky water, but Simon wasn't paying attention. He even told people his family drank sewer water at their house! When Mommy and Daddy found out, they were embarrassed that people thought they had dirty drinking water.

Simon didn't pay attention to what Daddy tried to explain to him. He ended up telling people wrong things. In the same way, you need to pay attention when your teacher or parents are telling you about God and the Bible. God wants you to tell people the right things about Him so others can be His friends, too.

Your Turn

1. What did Simon do wrong?

_____

_____

2. Why is it important to pay attention when you are learning about God and the Bible?

_____

_____

Prayer

God, please help me to remember that I should pay attention always, but especially when I am learning about You. Amen.

RAIN GAUGE

Read this to your child: "God wants you to pay attention when you are learning. If you don't pay attention, you might not learn the right things. Simon didn't pay attention when his daddy was talking, so he didn't learn about the different types of water. He also didn't learn that water can come from many places, such as deep in the ground or the sky when it rains. If you follow the directions below, you can make a rain gauge to measure how much water comes down the next time it rains at your house."

What You Need

glass jar
ruler
glue or tape

What to Do

1. Tape or glue a ruler to a glass jar.

2. Dig a 1- to 2-inch hole in an open spot of your yard (if the hole is under the roof or trees, you might not get an accurate reading). Placing the jar into the ground will prevent it from being tipped or blown over.

3. After it rains, check your jar to measure how many inches of rain fell.

4. Be sure to clean out your jar each time it rains so you start with an empty jar each rainfall.

DEVOTION

Jesus is my best friend.

Nor anything...will be able to separate us from the love of God.
– Romans 8:39

Charlie's Friends

The playground was full of kids playing football. Mitchell and his friend Charlie were having fun throwing the ball and running. But suddenly Mitchell turned around and saw Charlie lying on the ground. Charlie wasn't playing anymore. He was hurt.

The ball had hit Charlie in the mouth. His tooth was loose. As a grown-up took care of Charlie, Mitchell stayed by his side. When another of Charlie's friends came over, he simply asked, "You okay?" and then went back to playing. He didn't stay with Charlie like Mitchell did.

When Charlie was feeling better, Mitchell went home with him. He knew that he had done the right thing by staying with his friend.

Being a friend is more than just playing and having fun. It means taking care of each other during bad times, too. Jesus is a good friend to you like Mitchell was a good friend to Charlie. Jesus suffered and died for you even though there were lots of things that would have been more fun for Him to do. He did the right thing because He is your most important friend.

Your Turn

1. Are you always a good friend?

_____

_____

2. Who is your most important, best friend?

_____

_____

Prayer

Jesus, thank You for showing me what it's like to be a good friend. Please help me to remember to be a good friend to others as You are to me. Amen.

SCENTED CARDS

Read this to your child: "Jesus is your best friend. He died on the cross for you because He loves you so much. Being a good friend is about more than just having fun. Here's a way for you to show a friend how much you care."

What You Need

paper

scented extracts

cotton swabs

crayons

What to Do

1. Fold the paper in fourths like a greeting card.

2. Decorate the card in any way you like.

3. Dip the swab into the scented extract (vanilla, cherry and almond work well).

4. Use the swab to carefully "paint" along the inside and edges of your card.

5. You now have a yummy-scented card to show a family member or friend how much you care.

PATIENCE

God wants me to be patient.

Be patient with everyone.
– 1 Thessalonians 5:14

Baa-Baa Bottle

"More baa-baa," demanded baby Sean. "Baa-baa" was his way of saying "bottle" because he was just learning to talk.

"I think you should wait a little while," answered Mommy. Sean had already had two bottles of chocolate milk and it wasn't even lunchtime yet. Besides, Sean's bottle still had some milk in it.

"More baa-baa, more baa-baa," Sean said again, banging the bottle on the countertop. "More baa-baa now!"

"It's not good for you to have so much chocolate milk," said Mommy. "Wait until after lunch, and maybe you can have some more then."

"More baa-baa now!" Sean screamed. He slammed the bottle so hard on the counter that the top popped off and milk sprayed everywhere.

When you're not patient, bad things can happen. Sean wasn't patient about waiting for his milk. He got so mad about it that he made a mess and wasted the milk that he still had.

God wants you to be patient. That way, you have time to think about what is right instead of causing something bad to happen.

Your Turn

1. Have you ever caused something bad to happen because you were not patient?

_____

_____

2. Why does God want you to be patient?

_____

_____

Prayer

God, please help me to be patient, so I don't cause something bad to happen. Amen.

BAA-BAA BOTTLE

Read this to your child: "God wants you to be patient so that you don't cause something bad to happen. If you are patient and careful as you finish coloring the picture below, it could be very pretty."

MANIPULATION

God doesn't want me to hurt others to get what I want.

*By this all men will know that you are my disciples,
if you love one another.*
– John 13:35

Stop Talking!

Grandpa had come for a visit. Daddy was talking to Grandpa in the living room.

Alex didn't like that they were talking without him. He wanted Daddy to talk to him, and only him.

Alex tried to get Daddy's attention by talking to him, tugging on his pants and dancing around the room. But Daddy just kept talking to Grandpa.

Suddenly, Alex eyed the kitchen stool. He had an idea. He knew he wasn't supposed to stand on top of the stool, but he also knew that it would get Daddy's attention.

As Alex climbed onto the stool, Daddy and Grandpa stopped talking and hollered at Alex. Alex smiled. He finally had Daddy's attention.

It's not right to get what you want by doing something bad. Alex wanted his daddy to pay attention to him, but he wasn't nice about getting what he wanted. He used his daddy's fear for his safety to get him to pay attention to him. God doesn't want you to hurt others just to get what you want.

Your Turn

1. Have you ever done something bad just to get what you wanted?

_____

_____

2. Why is it wrong to do that?

_____

_____

Prayer

God, please help me to remember that it's not right to do something bad even if it will get me what I want. Amen.

DYE-DRIP TOWELS

Read this to your child: "God doesn't want you to do something bad just to get what you want. Here's a project that will get you what you want without doing something bad. If you fold the paper towel as described below a certain way, you'll get a pretty design."

What You Need

paper towels
food coloring

What to Do

1. Fold several paper towels, each in different ways (it doesn't matter how you do it).

2. Drop different colors of food coloring on the paper towels in various patterns. (Be sure to cover your work surface and clothing because food coloring can stain.)

3. Unfold the towels and let them dry. You'll see beautiful patterns!

DISCERNMENT

God wants me to discern between different situations and people.

The discerning heart seeks knowledge.

– Proverbs 15:14

Making Aidan Listen

"Why are you talking so loudly?" asked Mommy as Ashley was talking.

"Well," said Ashley, "that's because when I talk to Aidan, he doesn't always listen."

Aidan was Ashley's big brother. She loved to play with him.

"When I say 'Aidan, come here,'" Ashley said softly, "he doesn't even look at me.

"And then when I say 'Aidan, come here,'" Ashley said a little louder, "he just keeps riding his scooter."

"But when I say 'Aidan, come here,' just like this," Ashley nearly yelled, "he stops and says 'Ashley, what do you want?' So I have to talk like this!"

Ashley learned that talking loudly would cause people to listen to her better. She didn't realize, however, that she didn't always need to talk that loudly. Ashley needed to discern, or figure out, the difference between when she needed to talk loudly and when she didn't.

Many things in life take careful thought. You need to discern, or figure out, how to act in different situations and with different people. The Bible and your parents will help you to do that. But best of all, remember that God will always hear you, no matter how softly or loudly you talk to Him!

Your Turn

1. What do you do when you want someone to listen to you?

    _____

    _____

2. Who can always hear you, no matter what?

    _____

    _____

Prayer

Thank You, God, for always listening to me, even when I whisper. Amen.

WHAT'S DIFFERENT?

Read this to your child: "God has given you the Bible and your parents to help you know how to act in different situations. Look at the pictures below, and figure out what's different in each."

PROFANITY

I should only use God's name in good ways.

You shall not misuse the name of the Lord your God.
– Exodus 20:7

The "O" Word

"What's the 'D' word?" asked Nathaniel. He knew it was something bad, but he didn't know what it was. "Is it a cuss word?"

"Yes," answered Mommy. Then she explained what that word meant, and that Nathaniel should not say it.

"What about the 'S' word?" Nathaniel asked next. So Mommy explained that bad word to him, too.

When Mommy finished talking, Nathaniel frowned. There was still one thing he didn't understand.

"What's the 'O' word?" he asked.

Mommy looked confused. She didn't know what the "O" word was.

"What do you mean, Nathaniel?" she asked.

"You know," Nathaniel said, "when people say oh…my…"

"Do you mean the word 'God'?" asked Mommy as Nathaniel nodded. "It's always okay to say 'God' when you're talking to Him, or learning about Him. God just doesn't want us to use His name unless we're really talking about Him."

Just like swearing is wrong, it's wrong to use God's name in a bad way. His name should only be used in good ways.

Your Turn

1. When is it okay to say "God" or "Jesus"? When is it not okay?

_____

_____

2. Do you ever swear?

_____

_____

Prayer

God, please help me to remember that I should never swear or use Your name in a bad way. Amen.

PRAYING TO JESUS

Read this to your child: "God says that swearing is bad, so that's why you should never do it. You should only say God's name when you're talking about Him or to Him, like when you're praying. Cross out the picture below that shows when it is bad to use God's name. Circle the pictures that are good times to use God's name."

WARNINGS

I need to listen to God's warnings.

Do not be carried away by all kinds of strange teachings.
– Hebrews 13:9

When the Ice Melted

"Allie pulled my hair!" Ian complained to Mommy. Ian liked to play with Allie at preschool, but sometimes she got a little rough.

"Did you tell Mrs. Rowley?" asked Mommy. She was Ian's teacher.

"Yes, and she told Allie to stop it," answered Ian.

"Did Allie behave herself then?" asked Mommy.

"No," replied Ian. "Allie kept doing it. I told Mrs. Rowley that Allie pulled my hair again, and she said to Allie, 'You're on thin ice.'"

"What happened then?" Mommy asked.

"She did it again," said Ian, "so Mrs. Rowley called Allie's mommy."

Allie didn't learn by her mistake. Mrs. Rowley told her to stop pulling Ian's hair. Mrs. Rowley even warned Allie that she was going to be punished, but Allie still kept hurting Ian. Allie got in trouble with her mommy because she didn't listen to Mrs. Rowley's warning.

God gives you warnings just like Mrs. Rowley warned Allie. In the Bible, He warns you that bad things will happen to you if you do bad things. Learn about the Bible, and listen to God's warnings. God will help you live a good life so you don't have to worry about being punished.

Your Turn

1. Do you remember a time when you were warned to stop doing something bad? What happened?

_____

_____

2. Where does God warn about what will happen if we don't obey Him?

_____

_____

Prayer

God, please help me listen to Your warnings so that I don't do bad things. Amen.

SPROUTING BEANS

Read this to your child: "God gives you warnings to not do bad things in your life. You can learn what to do and what not to do from the Bible. You can learn how to do the project below by following the directions carefully. Can you guess what will happen if you keep the beans wet?"

What You Need

glass jar

paper towels

water

dried beans

What to Do

1. Line a glass jar with paper towels. Circle the towels around the sides so the bottom of the jar is empty.

2. Put about an inch of water in the bottom of the jar. The paper towels should touch the water.

3. Position the beans between the glass and the paper towels.

4. Don't let the paper towels dry out. In a few days you should begin to see both shoots and roots appear. You can now plant the beans in soil.

NORMALCY

God made me normal in my own way.

Let your light shine before men.

– Matthew 5:16

What's Normal?

"Why aren't we normal?" asked Cole.

"What do you mean by 'normal'?" asked Mommy with a frown.

"You know, like those kids there," Cole pointed to some kids walking down the street.

"What's so different about them?" Mommy asked.

Cole thought about it for a minute and answered, "Well, I'll bet they don't take baths in the sink or eat sap out of trees."

"Everyone does some things that might seem odd to others," explained Mommy. "Our washtub-sink is bigger than most sinks, so it's easier for little people like you to take a bath in. We make our own pancake syrup out of the sap we collect out of the maple trees. Other people might do those things, too. You just don't hear about it as much, but that doesn't mean that they're not normal."

Sometimes what you do might not seem 'normal.' But even if what you do is different, it doesn't mean that it's bad. God made each person special. You are normal in your very own way.

Your Turn

1. Can you think of some things your family does that might not seem "normal" to others?

_____

_____

2. Why does it not matter if you do things your own way?

_____

_____

Prayer

God, thank You for making me unique. Help me to remember that I'm normal in my own way. Amen.

COLLECTING SAP

Read this to your child: "God made you normal in your own way. Cole's family makes their own maple syrup, just like the kind you use on your pancakes. Not many people make their own syrup, but that's a normal thing for Cole's family to do. Here's a picture of Cole collecting sap for you to finish coloring."

RECYCLING

I can show I love God by caring for His world.

For we are God's fellow workers.

– 1 Corinthians 3:9

Recycling with Love

"Look at my picture book," called Micah. He had just spent a long time drawing with markers, so now Micah had a beautiful book of his work.

"Wow," said Daddy as he turned the pages. "These pictures are great!"

Micah's book had pictures of swings and pictures of people. There were even pictures of flowers and rainbows. But there was one picture that Daddy didn't understand.

"Tell me about this one," said Daddy.

"That picture is about recycling," said Micah proudly. His drawing showed red hearts with black X's through them. In the middle were black scribbles and lines, and a sad face was in the corner. "It's what the world would look like if everyone threw all their garbage on the ground and didn't clean up. We don't want the world to be a giant X, do we?"

"No, we don't Micah," answered Daddy. "That's a very good picture of recycling, and I especially like how the hearts show no love because they have X's through them."

God wants you to take good care of the world He has given you. That can mean recycling, or using things in more than one way. If you love God, you should love His world, too, and take care of it.

Your Turn

1. What do you recycle?

_____

_____

2. Why is it important to care for God's world?

_____

_____

Prayer

God, thank You for giving me this wonderful world to live in. Please help me to remember to keep it clean and pretty. Amen.

MILK CARTON FEEDER

Read this to your child: "God wants you to take good care of His world. Sometimes that means using things in more than one way. Here's a simple way that you can re-use a cardboard or plastic milk container for your feathered friends."

What You Need

empty milk carton
birdseed
craft stick
string

What to Do

1. Wash and dry the empty milk carton.

2. Punch a hole through the top and pull a string through it (to hang it).

3. Cut a 2- to 3-inch hole in the side of the container. The height of the hole determines how much seed you can place in your feeder.

4. Punch another hole below the opening to place a craft stick as a perch.

5. Fill with birdseed.

6. Hang your feeder and enjoy the birds!

SILLINESS

God likes when I am joyful.

I will continue with all of you for your...joy in the faith.
– Philippians 1:25

Silly Bumblebee

"There's a bumblebee as big as a wolf spider!" Cole screamed.

He loved to scare his little sister, Abby, when they played outside together.

"Not a wolf spider!" said Mommy as the children giggled.

"Okay then," Cole said, "as big as...the tongue of a shoe."

Abby giggled some more as she smiled up at Cole.

"Well," Abby said with a silly grin, "then it must have shoe laces."

"It doesn't have shoe laces!" Cole replied. "It's just like a tongue of a shoe."

Abby laughed as she spread her arms wide and ran in circles around Cole. "Oh, look, Cole," she said. "Here comes a big bumblebee with shoe laces. Buzz, buzz, buzz."

Cole watched as his sister "flew" around him. "Now I've seen everything," he said as he shook his head, smiling.

Cole started out being silly with his sister, but she ended up being even sillier than he was. It's fun to tell jokes and laugh. God wants you to be happy. He likes when you are silly and joyful.

Your Turn

1. Can you remember the last time you acted silly?

_____

_____

2. Why does God like for you to be happy?

_____

_____

Prayer

God, I'm glad that it's okay to be silly sometimes. Thank You for making me so happy. Amen.

CATCH CAN

Read this to your child: "God wants you to be happy, so it's okay to be silly sometimes. Here's a great way to be silly."

What You Need

plastic gallon-size milk carton

string

What to Do

1. Wash and dry the milk carton.

2. Cut off the bottom of a plastic milk carton, below the handle. Discard the bottom portion.

3. Punch a small hole at the bottom edge of the carton and tie a 2-inch string through it. Tie the opposite end around a balled-up piece of paper, balled-up piece of foil or any other small, soft item.

4. Holding the container by the handle, try to swing the ball up into the container. It's fun!

FIRE

God wants me to be safe.

Wisdom reposes in the heart of the discerning.

– Proverbs 14:33

Scary Fire

"Don't ever play with matches," Daddy said. He had been explaining fire to Cody and Samantha. "Fire is a dangerous thing. It can hurt you very badly."

"But it would only burn some things," said Cody.

"Yeah," Samantha agreed. "Fire would burn the wood and floor, but not dresses. I don't want my dress to get burnt."

"Not pretty dresses," said Cody. "Just other stuff."

Daddy was surprised Cody and Samantha didn't understand how fire works. "Fire doesn't just burn some things and not others," explained Daddy. "If you start a fire, it could spread and burn everything, and you wouldn't be able to stop it. That's why fire is so dangerous."

Cody and Samantha were so scared by what Daddy said that they got tears in their eyes. Fire sounded very scary to them.

Many of the things God gives can be used in good and bad ways. Fire is a good thing when it's used in good ways, like keeping you warm or cooking your food. Fire is bad when it's used to destroy things or hurt someone. God wants you to be safe. That means you should not play with fire.

Your Turn

1. Why should you never play with matches?

_____

_____

2. Why doesn't God want you to play with fire?

_____

_____

Prayer

God, thank You for giving us fire, but please help me to remember that it is very dangerous. I know You want me to be safe. Amen.

DOUBLE PUPPETS

Read this to your child: "Like fire, many of the things God gives you can be used in both good and bad ways. Here are some puppets you can make that could be used in both good and bad ways. You could use your puppet to scare your mommy, or to make her laugh. Which will you do?"

What You Need

construction paper

crayons

scissors

glue

What to Do

1. Fold a piece of construction paper into thirds, lengthwise.

2. Now fold the ends in to meet each other.

3. Bend the paper backward at the fold, so that you can stick your fingers into the two open ends.

4. Decorate your puppet.

5. You are ready to play!

ADVENTURESOME

God wants me to try new things.

So do not forsake my teaching.

– Proverbs 4:2

Robert Kool-Aid™

Grandma and Grandpa were spending the day with Joel. They were taking him to some of his favorite places. Joel loved to listen to his special tapes while they rode in the car.

After they had listened to Joel's kid tapes for a while, Grandpa said, "Okay, that's enough. We're playing our music for a little while now."

Joel didn't think he'd like Grandpa's music. *What if it's yucky?* he thought. *What if it's boring?*

Joel heard a man with a deep voice singing. "Who is that singing?" he asked.

"That's Robert Goulet," Grandma answered.

Joel listened for a long time. This wasn't what Joel had expected at all. This was good!

"Boy, I really like Robert Kool-Aid!" Joel said with a big smile.

Trying new things is good. If Joel hadn't tried listening to his grandparents' music, he would never have known how nice it was. By trying new things, you learn more about the world God has given you.

Your Turn

1. What was the last new thing you tried? Did you like it or not?

_____

_____

2. Why does God want you to try new things?

_____

_____

Prayer

God, thank You for making such a wonderful world where there is always something new to try. Amen.

NEW THINGS

Read this to your child: "God wants you to learn as much as you can, so that sometimes means trying new things, even if you think you won't like them. Below are some pictures of things that some people don't like to try. Circle the ones that you've tried. Ask your mommy or daddy to help you try those you haven't yet tried."

PAIN

God allows things to happen for a reason.

Blessed is the man who perseveres under trial.
– James 1:12

The Gift of Pain

"Ouch!" screamed Adrian. He had fallen on the driveway and now his knee was bleeding. "It hurts," he told Daddy with tears in his eyes.

"It's okay," said Daddy. "I'll take care of you, and you'll feel better soon."

"No, I won't!" cried Adrian. "I won't feel better! Why does it hurt? It's stupid that it has to hurt!"

Adrian didn't think it was right that he should have to feel pain. He didn't understand that pain can be a good thing sometimes. For example, if Adrian's knee didn't hurt, he wouldn't know that something was wrong. Also, because Adrian knows what it's like to feel pain, he can understand and help others who are hurt someday.

God allows things to happen for a reason. He knows what is best for you. The next time you feel pain, ask God to heal you. Then ask yourself what you are learning about God and His world because of that pain.

Your Turn

1. How is pain a good thing sometimes?

_____

_____

2. When was the last time you had pain? How was it good, and how was it bad?

_____

_____

Prayer

God, thank You for making pain a good thing sometimes, but please don't let me have to feel it very often. Amen.

CRAYON HOLDER

Read this to your child: "We can learn from everything God gives us, including pain. Here's an activity, however, that won't be painful. Just follow the directions and have fun."

What You Need

container

construction paper or fabric

glue

crayons or glitter

scissors

What to Do

1. Clean out an empty container. Nut cans work well.

2. Make sure there are no sharp spots (you can use a pliers to flatten raised edges).

3. Cut construction paper or fabric to fit the can, and glue it around it.

4. Decorate the can with crayons, glitter or whatever you like.

5. Now you have a beautiful crayon holder!

DEMANDS

God wants me to be thankful, not demanding.

Give thanks to the Lord.
– 1 Chronicles 16:34

Token Demands

Seth was having a great time at his friend's birthday party. He loved the balloons, pizza, cake…everything! All of his friends were with him as he chased and played in the fancy playground, running through the pretty tubes and throwing the fuzzy balls at the other kids. There were so many fun things to do that he couldn't decide what to do first, but that wasn't enough.

"When do I get some tokens?" Seth whined to his friend's mother. "I want tokens!

"There's lots of other things to do," she said. "You can do all the other things, you just can't play the games that take tokens."

"But I want tokens, too!" Seth cried.

Seth was very demanding. He had lots of things to do–so much, in fact, that there wasn't enough time to do them all. But even that wasn't enough.

God doesn't want you to be demanding like Seth was. God wants you to be thankful for the wonderful things He gives you.

Your Turn

1. Why did Seth want tokens?

_____

_____

2. Was there a time when you were demanding?

_____

_____

Prayer

God, thank You for all the wonderful things You have given me. Please help me remember to not be demanding. Amen.

SURPRISE BUNNY

Read this to your child: "God doesn't want you to be demanding. He wants you to be thankful for what you have. Some of the many things for which you can be thankful are the animals God created. Here's one to make that will surprise your friends."

What You Need

construction paper

scissors

foam cup

craft stick

glue or tape

What to Do

1. Draw or trace a bunny head on construction paper (make sure it's small enough to fit easily inside the cup).

2. Color or decorate the bunny and cut it out.

3. Attach the bunny to the top of a craft stick.

4. Punch a hole in the bottom of a cup.

5. Place the stick inside the cup and down through the hole in the bottom.

6. Make your bunny pop up out of the cup and surprise your friends!

LISTENING

God wants me to listen as well as talk.

Have the wisdom to show restraint.

– Proverbs 23:4

Too Much Talking

Devin never stopped talking. He talked all morning while he was getting dressed. He talked in the van, even when he was way in the back and no one could hear him. He talked when he was eating–with his mouth full! He even talked in his sleep, so that everyone in the house knew what he was dreaming. It seemed like Devin never stopped talking!

When Mommy would shush Devin, he would yell, "I wanna talk!" When Mommy timed Devin being quiet, he couldn't even make it for three minutes.

Devin talked so much, in fact, that he didn't take time to listen. He missed when Mommy said Grandma was coming to pick him up for an outing. He missed hearing about Daddy's fun day of shopping. He even missed hearing about how much Mommy loved the picture he drew for her. Devin missed a lot of things because he wouldn't stop talking.

God wants you to talk. It's good to tell how you feel and what you think. It's not good, however, to talk so much that you forget to listen. God wants you to listen, too, because listening is sometimes more important than talking. It's by listening that you learn and can help others.

Your Turn

1. Do you talk more, or listen more?

_____

_____

2. Why does God want you to listen and talk?

_____

_____

Prayer

God, please help me to remember that even though talking is okay, I need to listen, too. Amen.

BUZZING BEES

Read this to your child: "Talking can be lots of fun, but God wants you to listen, too. God wants you to learn and grow, and you can do that best by listening more than talking. Another great thing about listening is that you can hear all the wonderful sounds of nature, like the buzzing of bees. Here's a way to make your own bee."

What You Need

empty egg carton

chenille wire

markers

construction paper

tape or glue

What to Do

1. Cut out three connected sections of an egg carton.

2. Color the sections yellow and black.

3. Draw wings on construction paper and cut them out.

4. Tape or glue the wings to the egg carton "body."

5. Stick two pieces of chenille wire into the body for antenna.

THOUGHTFULNESS

God wants me to think of others.

Always try to be kind to each other and to everyone else.
– 1 Thessalonians 5:15

Stones for Anna

Paul loved shopping with his mommy. It was really special when he and Mommy were together, just the two of them. When they went into a store that had pretty stones, Paul remembered the last time he was there with his whole family. His little sister, Anna, had loved the stones.

"I want to get some pretty stones for Anna's birthday," Paul told Mommy. "You can take the money for them out of my bank." Paul had his own bank account where he saved the money he earned doing chores around the house.

Paul bought the stones, wrapped them and saved them until it was time for his sister's birthday. He was so happy and proud to be able to give Anna a gift that was just from him.

Paul remembered not only his sister's birthday, but even the stones he knew she'd like. He even gave up his money, something for which he had worked hard, to buy the stones for Anna. Paul was very thoughtful toward his sister. God wants you to be thoughtful, too.

Your Turn

1. Have you ever gotten a gift for someone special?

_____

_____

2. Why does God want you to be thoughtful?

_____

_____

Prayer

God, please help me to be thoughtful so, like You, I can bring happiness to others. Amen.

HELPING OTHERS

Read this to your child: "God wants you to think of others and do what you can to help them. Below are some ways to help others. Look at the pictures, then fill in the empty square with your own idea of how to help others."

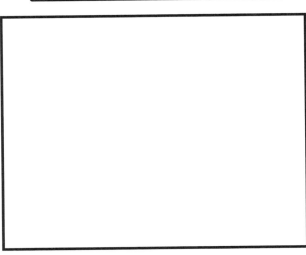

COURTESY

God wants me to be nice to others.

Live at peace with everyone.

– Romans 12:18

Mailing Fudge

The store smelled wonderful! All around Lucas there were rows and rows of fudge of every type and flavor.

Lucas was surprised that he and Mommy were the only ones in the store. The young man behind the counter looked like he was bored because there was no one with whom he could talk.

"Can I help you?" the man asked, but Mommy told him she didn't need help. He looked sad, Lucas thought, like he was disappointed he couldn't help.

As they started to leave, Mommy turned to the man and asked if the store could mail fudge to people as gifts. Lucas noticed that the man seemed happier as he talked with Mommy about mailing fudge.

After they left the store, Lucas asked, "Are we going to buy some fudge to mail to someone?"

"No," said Mommy. "I noticed that the young man looked eager to help. I asked him a question as a courtesy just so he would feel needed."

Lucas's mommy didn't have to ask the man a question. She asked him about mailing fudge simply because it was a nice thing to do. It was a courtesy. In the same way, God wants you to be nice to people, even if it doesn't affect you. Find ways to show courtesy.

Your Turn

1. Can you remember the last time you did something just to be nice?

_____

_____

2. Why does God want you to be courteous?

_____

_____

Prayer

God, please help me to remember to find ways to be courteous. Amen.

MAILING FUDGE

Read this to your child: "God wants you to be nice to other people. If Lucas had mailed some fudge to a friend, that would have been a way to be nice to someone. Look at the maze below. Can you help the fudge find its way to Lucas's friend's house?"

ANTICIPATION

Only God knows what will happen in my life.

Trust in the Lord forever.

– Isaiah 26:4

Shopping Fun

"I don't want to go," said Blake.

Mommy was taking Blake's sister to a birthday party. Mommy told Blake if he came along, he and Mommy could go shopping while they waited for the party to end. But now he had changed his mind.

"But you always like to go shopping," answered Mommy.

"I know, but not this time," Blake said. He was mad because he wasn't invited to the party. He figured if he couldn't go to the party, then he couldn't have fun doing anything else either.

"Well, just come with me anyway," Mommy urged.

As Blake rode to the store with Mommy, he was still mad. But after visiting a couple of stores, Blake found that he wasn't thinking so much about the party anymore. His thoughts were more on shopping with Mommy, and less on the party he was missing. Before long, Blake was laughing and having a wonderful time.

Sometimes things don't turn out the way you might anticipate. Only God knows exactly what will happen in your life. You might think it will go a certain way, but it might not. It is your job to make the best of whatever happens, and thank God that He has a special plan just for you.

Your Turn

1. Have you ever been so angry that you let it keep you from having fun?

_____

_____

2. What does God want you to do instead of being angry?

_____

_____

Prayer

God, please help me to remember that only You know what will happen in my life. Amen.

TRICKY DOLLAR

Read this to your child: "What you anticipate doesn't always come true. Blake almost let his sadness about the party keep him from having fun with Mommy. Here's something that seems like it won't work, but try it and you'll see that it does."

What You Need

crisp dollar bill

quarter

What to Do

1. Fold the dollar bill in half.

2. Place the quarter at the fold, balancing it there.

3. Slowly pull the two ends apart until the dollar bill is straight. If you do it very slowly and carefully enough, the quarter won't fall.

DETAILS

Knowing the Bible will help me to keep my life straight.

The message is heard through the word of Christ.

– Romans 10:17

Getting It Straight

"They're gone," cried Trevor. "Someone took my cards!"

Trevor had taken his trading cards to day care with him. On his way home, he noticed that 10 were missing.

Daddy and Trevor talked about where Trevor was and where the cards were at any given time that day. After lunch, Trevor said, he had put the cards in his cubby and never took them out again until it was time to go home. Daddy went over it with him again and again to make sure they had it straight.

"So after putting them in your cubby, what did you do?" Daddy asked.

"I went to lunch," said Trevor. His little brother, Jesse, giggled. Even he remembered that Trevor had said he put the cards in his cubby after lunch. But now Trevor thought he put the cards in his cubby before lunch. He wasn't sure what had really happened!

It's important to get all of the details. Knowing how things happened can help you figure out the truth. In the same way, knowing the details of the Bible and how God wants you to live will help you keep your life straight.

Your Turn

1. Think of the last time you went somewhere. Can you remember the details of what happened?

   _____

   _____

2. Why does God want you to know what the Bible says?

   _____

   _____

Prayer

God, thank You for the Bible so I can know how to live for You. Amen.

BALANCING ACT

Read this to your child: "The details of the Bible will help you to live a good and happy life. In the same way, if you follow the directions for this activity, you will have fun. Finish coloring the picture when you're done."

What You Need

clean spoons

What to Do

1. Breathe onto the spoon until it's moist.

2. Immediately press the spoon against your nose and hold it for a moment, then let go. The spoon should stay in place all by itself!

FRUSTRATION

I should ask for help when I am frustrated.

Come to me, all you who are...burdened.

– Matthew 11:28

Not Now!

"Where's my watch?" yelled Mommy. She always kept her watch in the same place by the door so it would be easy to find.

"Who took my watch?" Mommy yelled again.

"Mommy," Jared said softly from behind Mommy, but Mommy didn't hear him. Mommy was still yelling about someone taking her watch.

"Mommy?" Jared said again, louder this time.

"Not now!" Mommy answered.

"But Mommy…"

"Oh what is it?" Mommy finally said.

"Your watch is right there, under your purse," Jared said.

Mommy looked where Jared said. Sure enough, her watch had been there all along, hidden under her purse. Mommy had allowed her frustration at not being able to find her watch keep her from listening to Jared. If she had just listened, she would have found the watch sooner.

"I'm sorry for getting angry," said Mommy as she hugged Jared.

God understands that everyone gets frustrated sometimes. That's why He gives you other people to help you. The next time you are frustrated, ask for some help. If no one is around, ask God for help. If you act badly when you are frustrated, apologize to the people you may have hurt.

Your Turn

1. Tell about a time when you were frustrated.

_____

_____

2. What can you do when you get frustrated?

_____

_____

Prayer

God, please help me to remember when I'm frustrated, I should ask for help. Amen.

TWO THINGS AT ONCE

Read this to your child: "Everyone gets frustrated sometimes, but God doesn't want you to let that frustration keep you from being nice. Here's a fun, but frustrating, activity to try: rub your stomach in a circular pattern with your hand, while patting the top of your head with your other hand at the same time.

RELAXATION

God can help me relax.

The Lord is my helper; I will not be afraid.
                                        – Hebrews 13:6

Freaking Out

"I don't know how I'm going to get this all done," Mommy said as she hurried around the kitchen. She was trying to make dinner and get ready for a speech she was giving that night.

Chase watched Mommy rush around as he ate his crackers. He could see that she was upset, and he knew what to do to calm Mommy down.

Chase quietly crept up behind Mommy. He carefully placed his hand on her back and rubbed it lightly.

When Mommy felt his hand, she jumped and said, "Not now, Chase!" But Chase kept rubbing.

After a short time, Mommy finally began to slow down and relax.

"Thank you, Chase," Mommy said as she turned to hug him. "How did you know just what I needed?"

"You were freaking out," Chase simply said.

Chase knew that rubbing his mommy's back would calm her down. The nice feeling on her back helped her to relax. God is like getting a rub on your back. His love and His words in the Bible can help you relax when you're upset. God promises to love and care for you so you will feel better.

Your Turn

1. How did Chase help his mommy relax?

_____

_____

2. How is God like a rub on your back?

_____

_____

Prayer

God, thank You for Your love and care. Knowing You are with me always helps me to feel better. Amen.

WIGGLY WORM

Read this to your child: "Knowing God loves you and will always care for you can help you relax. Here's an activity where you can make a paper worm relax. Just follow the directions below."

What You Need
paper-wrapped drinking straw

What to Do

1. Stand the paper-wrapped straw on its end.

2. Holding onto the top, push the wrapper all the way down to the table and remove the straw. You have made a paper worm!

3. To make your worm wiggle, drip a tiny drop of water off of your finger onto the worm.

INITIATIVE

God wants me to speak up when it is right.

Clothe yourselves with compassion.

– Colossians 3:12

No Popcorn

"Where's your popcorn?" Mommy asked as Richard stepped off the bus.

"I didn't get any," Richard said tearfully. Richard's kindergarten teacher, Mrs. Hudson, had said there would be popcorn for 25 cents at school that day. Richard had been so excited that morning! He had checked his pocket three times to make sure he had the money.

"Did they run out of popcorn?" Mommy asked.

"No, they didn't run out," Richard cried. "Mrs. Hudson just said that I couldn't have any."

"Did you cry?" Mommy asked.

"No," Richard answered, "I was just very sad."

Richard thought it wasn't his fault that he didn't get any popcorn. But when Mommy spoke with Mrs. Hudson, she said she didn't know Richard had money with him. If Richard had given Mrs. Hudson his quarter, and explained how he felt, things may have turned out differently.

Richard didn't step forward and speak up for what he wanted, so he didn't get any popcorn. He didn't take initiative.

God wants you to speak up when it is the right thing to do. He especially wants you to tell others about His love. God wants you to take initiative.

Your Turn

1. Can you remember a time when you had to speak for yourself?

_____

_____

2. Why does God want you to take initiative?

_____

_____

Prayer

Thank You, God, for taking care of me. Help me to remember that sometimes I need to take charge, too. Amen.

POPCORN PICTURE

Read this to your child: "God is always with you, loving and caring for you, but sometimes you need to speak up for yourself, too. Here's something you can do yourself. Finish coloring the picture any way you like."

IMPATIENCE

God wants me to be patient.

All that the Father gives me will come to me.
– John 6:37

Where's Lunch?

"Where's my lunch!?" yelled Dakota. He had just come home from preschool and he wanted to eat.

"It's not ready yet," said Mommy. "I know you like to eat right away when you get home, but I just got home, too, and haven't had time to cook yet."

"Arghhh," yelled Dakota as he stomped his feet. "Why is my lunch never ready when I get home?"

Dakota threw his backpack down on the floor and stomped over to his stool at the table. As he jumped up onto the stool, Dakota pounded his fists on the table and yelled, "I want to eat now!"

Dakota pounded his fists so hard, in fact, that he lost his balance and fell right off the stool and onto the floor. Dakota cried. He was hurt and scared from his fall, but it taught him to be much more patient in the future.

Dakota wanted lunch ready when he got home. He was impatient with his mommy–he didn't want to wait for Mommy to make something, and that wasn't nice.

God wants you to be patient with other people, just as you would want them to be patient with you. That's God's way.

Your Turn

1. How does God want you to behave?

_____

_____

2. Can you remember a time when you were impatient? What happened?

_____

_____

Prayer

God, please help me to remember that I should be patient with people, just as You are patient with me. Amen.

DAKOTA'S LUNCH

Read this to your child: "God wants you to be patient with others. It's just one of many ways that you can be like Him, because God is patient with you, too. If you are patient going through the maze below, you'll help Dakota find his way to the end so he can eat his lunch."

FALLIBILITY

Everyone fails sometimes.

We are God's children.

– Romans 8:16

The Gardening Boy

Mommy called Dominic "Gardening Boy" because, of the four children in his family, Dominic was the only one who loved to garden.

Dominic even had his own garden. During the summer, he grew carrots, corn and flowers. Everything he planted grew.

When Dominic's school decided to grow bean seeds in cups, Dominic was very excited. He just knew that his bean plant would grow higher and better than all the others. After all, he was the Gardening Boy.

However, when all the plants had grown so tall that it was time to take them home, Dominic's was the only cup in which there was no plant.

When Mommy picked up Dominic from preschool, she started to laugh. She just couldn't help it! Of all the cups, how could Gardening Boy's bean not grow? Dominic looked at his mommy and frowned, but after he thought about it, he grinned, too. It was kind of funny that his was the only plant that wouldn't grow!

No one can do everything right all the time. Even a Gardening Boy like Dominic had things go wrong. Like Dominic, no matter how good you are, you will make mistakes sometimes. Only God is perfect.

Your Turn

1. What happened to Dominic's bean plant?

_____

_____

2. Do you make mistakes sometimes?

_____

_____

Prayer

God, I know I'll make mistakes sometimes, but that's okay as long as I always try my best. Amen.

HELPFUL INSECTS

Read this to your child: "Only God is perfect. You will make mistakes sometimes, but that's okay. Even Dominic's beautiful garden needs help from nature sometimes. Below are pictures of insects that help gardens, and some that can hurt them. Can you tell which is which? Circle the helpers and draw an X through the harmers." (Parents: the only harmer below is the grasshopper. The other three are helpers.)

WASTEFULNESS

It is wrong to waste what God gives me.

Anyone, then, who knows the good he ought
to do and doesn't do it, sins.

– James 4:17

Something Fishy

"I want more! I want more!" yelled Jeremiah.

Mommy had made a fancy fish dinner. Even though Mommy said she could make Jeremiah something else, he insisted on eating fish, too.

"Okay, Jeremiah," Mommy said, "you can have the last piece of fish, but since you asked for it, I expect you to eat it. You'd better not waste any." Jeremiah still complained that his piece of fish wasn't big enough, but he nodded his head.

Later, Daddy noticed Jeremiah's piece of fish was in the dog's dish. Jeremiah hadn't eaten his fish after all. He had wasted his fish even though he had complained that he wanted more. Daddy later found out that Jeremiah gave his fish to the dog not because he didn't like it, but because he was mad that he hadn't been given a bigger piece.

God doesn't want you to be wasteful on purpose. Even if you're mad like Jeremiah was, it's not okay to waste things. God wants you to make the best use of all He gives you.

Your Turn

1. Can you think of something that you once wasted?

_____

_____

2. Why is it wrong to waste what God gives you?

_____

_____

Prayer

God, thank You for all the wonderful things You give me. Please help me to never be wasteful. Amen.

WASTEFULNESS

Read this to your child: "God doesn't want you to be wasteful of all the wonderful things He has given you. Look at each picture below. How is the boy being wasteful? What are some ways he could be less wasteful?"

NICENESS

God wants me to be nice to others.

Let your gentleness be evident to all.
– Philippians 4:5

Naughty Ricky

Jaden loved everything about Sunday school. He loved making the fun crafts and singing songs. He loved hearing the stories from the Bible. Most of all, he loved learning about Jesus.

Yes, Jaden usually loved Sunday school…but not today. Today, Jaden had cried during Sunday school.

"Ricky hurt my hand," Jaden cried as he told Daddy what happened to him. "When Teacher said we should shake hands, Ricky squeezed my hand sooo tight. I told him to stop, but he just kept squeezing. It hurt."

"Did you tell your teacher what happened?" Daddy asked as he hugged Jaden close.

"I told Teacher, and she made Ricky say he was sorry." Jaden said. Then he added, "What Ricky did wasn't very nice!"

Ricky wasn't nice to Jaden. He hurt Jaden instead of being loving toward him as God would have wanted him to be. You should never be mean like Ricky was. God wants you to be nice to others.

Your Turn

1. What did Jaden not like about Sunday school on this day?

_____

_____

2. Have you ever not been nice to someone? Why or why not?

_____

_____

Prayer

God, please help me to always be nice to others. Amen.

THUMB CRITTERS

Read this to your child: "God wants you to be nice to other people. It's an important part of being a Christian. Here's something fun to do. After you make them, it would be 'nice' for you to give them to someone as a present."

What You Need

paper

colored pencils or pens

chocolate sauce, mustard or ketchup

What to Do

1. Dip the child's thumb or finger into the sauce.

2. Press it down on paper. You may have to practice a few times to get the right consistency of sauce to make a clear print.

3. After you practice making prints, add a few details to make them into cute critters as shown.

4. Show how to make prints on plain paper to use as notepaper or gift wrap.

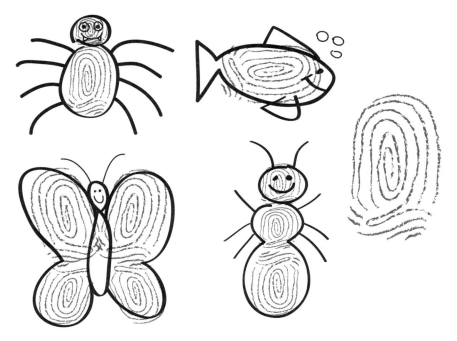

WATCHFULNESS

God wants me to be watchful of my behavior.

Make every effort to be found spotless.

– 2 Peter 3:14

Watching Hummingbirds

"Keep watching," Mommy told Jesse as they sat very still on the porch bench. A plastic bottle filled with red liquid was hanging above them. Every so often, a very tiny bird called a hummingbird would whiz by to take a quick drink from it.

"If you sit very still and quiet," Mommy whispered, "you'll see the hummingbird come for another drink."

It took a few minutes, but sure enough, the beautiful bird came to drink again. The little bird hovered by the bottle, sticking his long, thin beak into the liquid again and again as he drank. It had been difficult for Jesse to sit so still and quiet, but it was worth it to see such a pretty sight.

God wants you to be watchful, too, only He wants you to be watchful of your own behavior. God wants you to be careful to do the right thing and live your life the way the Bible teaches. As Jesse had difficulty sitting quietly, it may not always be easy to be watchful of your behavior, but it will be worth it. By watching what you do, you'll be better able to act as God wants.

Your Turn

1. Do you remember a time when you saw (or did) something special because you were still and quiet?

   _____

   _____

2. Why does God want you to be watchful of your behavior?

   _____

   _____

Prayer

God, please help me to be watchful of my behavior, so that I do the kinds of things You would want me to do. Amen.

HUMMINGBIRD

Read this to your child: "God wants you to be watchful of your behavior. Have you ever seen a hummingbird? Here is a picture of Jesse's hummingbird for you to finish coloring."

CONSTANCY

God loves and cares for me, no matter what.

How great is the love the Father has lavished on us.
– 1 John 3:1

Alejandro's Loose Tooth

Mommy wanted Daddy to pull out Alejandro's tooth. Mommy was afraid that if they didn't pull it out, Alejandro might swallow it by accident.

"Are you sure you want me to pull it out?" Daddy asked Alejandro. Alejandro nodded quickly. He couldn't wait for his tooth to come out so that he could put it under his pillow for the Tooth Fairy.

Alejandro stood very still in front of Daddy and opened his mouth wide as Daddy gripped the loose tooth with his fingers. Daddy was still for a moment, and then suddenly he pulled very hard, and very fast and… pop, the tooth came out…and Alejandro swallowed it!

"My tooth!" Alejandro cried. He cried and cried. Alejandro was afraid that if he didn't have his tooth to put under his pillow, the Tooth Fairy wouldn't leave him any money. But that night, the Tooth Fairy came anyway, leaving 100 pennies under his pillow. Alejandro was very happy.

The Tooth Fairy came even though Alejandro didn't have his tooth. It didn't matter. In the same way, God will always love and care for you. It doesn't matter to Him how you dress or where you live, or even how many teeth you have. He will always be there for you. You can count on Him to love and care for you, no matter what.

Your Turn

1. Why did Alejandro cry after his tooth came out?

_____

_____

2. What are some thing you can always count on?

_____

_____

Prayer

God, thank You for always being there for me. I know I can count on You and Your love. Amen.

ALEJANDRO'S PARENTS

Read this to your child: "God's love will always be there for you. You can always count on Him! Another thing you can count is pennies. Count the pennies in each row below. Write the number at the end of the row."

 _____

 _____

_____

STRESS MANAGEMENT

God's love helps me feel better.

Do not be anxious about anything.
– Philippians 4:6

Quarter Chicken

"Mark's a half-chicken," Olivia told Mommy as Olivia waited her turn at the dentist's office.

Her big brother, Mark, had gone in for his appointment first. Mark and Olivia both had cavities that needed to be filled, but Olivia wasn't as afraid as Mark.

"I'm only a quarter-chicken," she said, "because I have pony memories in my mind."

"What do you mean?" asked Mommy.

"I can think of ponies and not be afraid," Olivia explained, "but Mark only thinks about exploding things, so that doesn't help much."

Olivia had learned a way to make herself feel less afraid. When she was frightened, she would just think about ponies and nice things, and then she wouldn't feel so afraid anymore.

Jesus is like that. Praying to Him or singing songs about Him can make you feel better. When you're very afraid, you can think of Jesus and how He's always with you, so you don't need to feel all alone and afraid anymore.

Your Turn

1. Why was Olivia less scared than Mark?

_____

_____

2. What can you do to feel better when you're afraid?

_____

_____

Prayer

God, please help me to remember that You are always with me so I can feel less afraid. Amen.

BUTTERFLY OR MOTH?

Read this to your child: "Thinking about God and how He's always with you and loves you can make you feel better when you're afraid. Thinking about beautiful things like ponies, rainbows and butterflies can also help. Here's something nice to think, and learn, about: what's the difference between a moth and a butterfly?"

1. Which antenna is a butterfly?

2. Which picture is of a butterfly sitting down?

 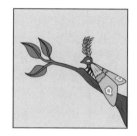

3. Do butterflies fly around during the day or night?

Answers:

1. A moth has feathery antenna and they're also thicker.
2. A butterfly's wings are vertical, a moth's horizontal.
3. Butterflies are out during the day, moths at night.

REPUTATION

God wants me to tell the truth.

You shall not give false testimony against your neighbor.
– Exodus 20:16

Garrett's Lies

"It's real easy to trick Alyssa," said Garrett.

"What do you mean?" asked Mommy.

"Like last night," Garrett began, "I told Alyssa, 'Hey, Daddy brought you egg-drop soup' and Alyssa ran downstairs, but there wasn't any."

"That wasn't nice," said Mommy with a frown. "If you lie to people, they won't believe what you tell them anymore, even when it's true. You start to be known as someone who lies all the time."

Garrett thought about what Mommy said. "When I told Alyssa that Daddy had egg-drop soup today," he said, "she didn't believe me. But he really had brought soup today."

"You see," Mommy said, "now Alyssa thinks that you lie, so she's not going to believe you anymore."

If people catch you lying, they probably won't believe anything you say, even when you're telling the truth. God doesn't want you to lie.

Your Turn

1. Why didn't Alyssa believe Garrett the second time he told her there was soup?

_____

_____

2. Why does God want you not to lie?

_____

_____

Prayer

Dear God, please help me to remember that I should never lie. Amen.

DOORKNOB REMINDER

Read this to your child: "God says you should never lie. You should always tell the truth. Here's a project that you can hang on your bedroom doorknob to remind you to always tell the truth. You can color the picture below when you're done."

What You Need

cardboard or paper

scissors

crayons

What to Do

1. Cut out a shape like the one shown.

2. Write "Truth" on it.

3. Color it any way you like to remind you of what you need to remember.

4. Punch a hole in the top to fit your doorknob.

5. When you're done, just hang it on your doorknob so you'll see it all the time!

PRIVACY

God wants me to respect the privacy of others.

Do to others what you would have them do to you.
– Matthew 7:12

Listening In

"Where is Owen?" Daddy said to himself. Owen's older brother, Joe, was playing soccer so Daddy and Owen had come to watch.

But where was Owen?

Daddy looked all around the soccer field, but he couldn't see Owen anywhere. Then suddenly there was a thump. Daddy turned to see little Owen drop out of a pine tree nearby.

"What were you doing up there?" Daddy asked.

"I was spying on the girls," Owen said. He had climbed high into the tree and sat very quietly so the girls didn't know he was there. He listened to what they said. Owen was quite proud of himself that they didn't even know that he was listening.

When Joe heard what Owen had done, he was surprised. "That wasn't very nice," he said. "You shouldn't listen in on what other people are saying unless they want you to. It's not right."

Owen was wrong to spy on the girls. Just as you sometimes like privacy, so do other people. God wants you to respect people's privacy.

Your Turn

1. When do you like privacy?

_____

_____

2. Why is it wrong to spy on others?

_____

_____

Prayer

God, please help me to remember that I shouldn't listen in on other people's conversations. Amen.

OWEN'S TREE

Read this to your child: "God wants you to respect each person's privacy. Owen should have been watching the soccer game instead. Do you like soccer? What sport do you like? Draw a line from the sports ball below to what goes with it."

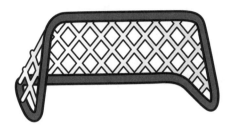

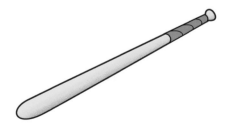

ATTITUDE

God wants me to have a good attitude about good things.

Rejoice in the Lord always.

– Philippians 4:4

Playing Ball

Xavier didn't want to play ball with the other kids. He liked to play ball, and he liked the other kids, he just didn't feel like playing ball today. But he did it anyway because Mommy told him he should.

When the game was over, Mommy asked Xavier if he had fun. "It was okay," Xavier said, "but I don't want to play again tomorrow."

"Why not?" asked Mommy.

"It's too hot and sweaty out there," said Xavier, pointing to the field.

"But you played so well!" Mommy said as she gave Xavier a big hug. "In fact, if you play again tomorrow, I'll come and watch the whole game, and I'll even bring some snacks so we can have a little picnic after you're done playing."

When Xavier heard that Mommy would come watch him, he changed his mind about playing. From that day on, playing ball, even though it was hot and sweaty, was a lot of fun.

Xavier's "attitude" about playing ball changed after he heard Mommy would come watch him. Once he had a good attitude about playing ball, he found that it was fun after all. God wants you to have a good attitude about your life. He wants you to try your best to feel good about doing the right things.

Your Turn

1. What made Xavier change his mind about playing ball?

_____

_____

2. Why does God want you to have a good attitude?

_____

_____

Prayer

God, please help me to have a good attitude about what I do in life. Amen.

PRETTY LANTERN

Read this to your child: "God wants you to have a good attitude. Here's a project that may seem hard to do at first, but if you have a good attitude about it, it will turn out just fine."

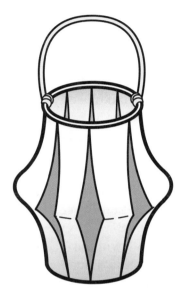

What You Need

paper

crayons

scissors

tape

string

What to Do

1. Color a piece of paper.

2. Fold the paper in half lengthwise and cut slits along the folded edge (but not all the way across to the unfolded edge).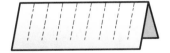

3. Unfold the paper, roll it into a tube-shape and tape the edges together.

4. Punch holes in the top and use a string to hang your lantern.

INDEPENDENCE

All I really need is God's love.

And my God will meet all your needs.

– Philippians 4:19

Where's Teddy

"Where's Teddy?" asked Bryce. He had just gone to bed and he couldn't find his teddy bear anywhere.

"I don't know," answered Daddy, "did you look everywhere?"

"Yeah, I even looked in the basement, but I can't find him," Bryce said with tears in his eyes. "I need him to fall asleep."

"You know what?" said Daddy. "I'll bet Teddy just wanted to sleep somewhere else tonight. I'll bet he's having a sleepover somewhere. Let's let him have fun, and you can sleep without him tonight."

"I don't think I can," said Bryce. "I always fall asleep with Teddy."

A few tears fell from Bryce's eyes, but he held Daddy's hand tight. Soon he was fast asleep…without Teddy by his side.

Bryce thought he couldn't sleep without Teddy, but he learned that he didn't really need Teddy after all. Just holding Daddy's hand was enough to make him feel safe and secure, and he soon slept just fine.

Sometimes the things you think you need aren't really as important as you think they are. Teddy bears, blankets and favorite toys are nice, but all you really need is God's love.

Your Turn

1. What do you need?

_____

_____

2. Why is God's love all you really need?

_____

_____

Prayer

God, thank You for Your love, which is all I ever really need. Amen.

FISHY REMINDER

Read this to your child: "All you really need is God's love. The fish symbol, called an 'ichthus,' can be a reminder of God just like a cross can. If you color just the circles and triangles below, you'll see the fish (turn the book sideways to see it better."

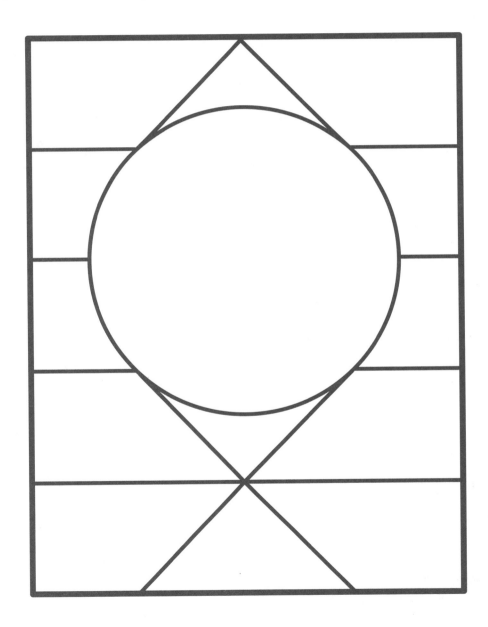

CREATIVITY

I should use the creativity God gives me.

See to it, then, that the light within you is not darkness.
– Luke 11:35

The Brick Road

"Follow the yellow brick road," the boys sang over and over from the living room.

"What are you doing?" Mommy called from the other room.

"We're skipping down the road we made," Benjamin said.

When Mommy peeked into the living room, she was surprised at what she saw. Mommy had vacuumed the living room that morning. When she was finished, she had pulled the vacuum through the room to put it away. The wheels left a track in the thick carpeting that looked like a road, so the boys were playing on it.

"That's so neat," said Mommy as she watched the boys use their blocks to fill in the "brick" road. Benjamin drove his cars down the road, and his brother drew pretend street signs with his finger into the rug next to their road. They even pretended that they were cars as they "vroom-vroomed" down their road. Before they were done, the boys had played on their pretend road for over an hour.

Sometimes even the simplest of things can be made into something fun. God made you a smart and creative person. If you use the creativity God gave you, you can make up all kinds of fun and useful things to do.

Your Turn

1. When have you used your creativity?

_____

_____

2. Who gives you creativity?

_____

_____

Prayer

God, thank You for giving me creativity. Please help me to use it wisely. Amen.

RACING CAR

Read this to your child: "God gives you creativity, but it's up to you to use it wisely. You get two chances below to use your creativity. Finish coloring the pictures any way you like."

URGENCY

I can trust God when I feel urgency.

Accept the word planted in you.

– James 1:21

Where's Mommy?

"Where's Mommy?" Diego said to himself. He had been chasing around the room with his play group when his head started to hurt. Even though he sat down for a while, his head still kept hurting…and then his throat hurt…and then his whole body started to hurt.

A grown-up had called his mommy, but why wasn't she there yet?

Mommy had told Diego that she was only a few minutes away if he needed her, but it seemed like it had been a long time since she was called. As he rubbed his head with his hands, Diego wondered where she was. Maybe she was too busy to come get him. Maybe Mommy decided to go shopping before coming to get him.

As Diego thought of all the things Mommy might be doing instead of picking him up, he started to cry. Then Diego heard a voice in the hallway.

"Mommy!" Diego cried as he ran into his mommy's outstretched arms.

It can seem important for some things to happen right away. Diego wanted his mommy as soon as he felt sick, but it took a few minutes for her to get there. When you want something to happen, ask God to help you be calm and patient. Trust God to take care of you.

Your Turn

1. Do you remember a time when you got upset because something didn't happen fast enough?

_____

_____

2. Who can you trust to help you be calm and patient?

_____

_____

Prayer

God, please help me to trust in You. I know You will take care of me. Amen.

FEELING BETTER

Read this to your child: "You should trust in God to help you be calm and patient. Below are some things Diego's mommy used to make him feel better after they got home. You can finish coloring the pictures, then talk with your mommy and daddy about how each one can be used to make you feel better."

FABRICATION

God wants me to know how His world works.

Your law is true.

– Psalm 119:142

The Moon and the Sun

"Look at that," said Lauren as she pointed out the van window. "I can see both the moon and the sun at the same time."

"How come we can see the moon in the morning?" asked Lauren's brother, Riley.

Mommy started to answer, but Lauren quickly cut in saying, "I know, I know. It's because the moon and the sun are friends, and they want to see each other."

"Maybe they want to shake hands," added Riley.

"Well, actually," said Mommy, "it's just because it's very early in the morning, and not very light out yet–that's why you can see both. As it gets more light out, you won't be able to see the moon anymore."

Lauren and Riley didn't understand why they could see both the moon and sun at the same time, so they made up a story that made sense to them. But that didn't make it true. Even though their story was fun, it wasn't the real reason for seeing the moon and sun at the same time.

God wants you to understand the world He made. It's okay to make up stories about how things work, but only if it's just for fun. You should still learn the real ways that God's world works.

Your Turn

1. Do you ever make up silly stories to explain how things work?

_____

_____

2. Why is it important to learn how God's world works?

_____

_____

Prayer

God, thank You for making me so creative that I can make up stories, but thanks for making me smart enough to learn the truth, too. Amen.

FILL-IN STORY

Read this to your child: "God wants you to learn how things really work. Here's a story you can make yourself–and it's true, too. You can color the picture when you're done."

Parents: Read the story below, letting your child fill in the missing words by guessing the meaning of the symbols.

God [heart] U so much that He sent His [sun] to die on the [cross] for U. It's because Jesus [rose] from the dead that U

are saved from your sins.

Answer: God <u>loves</u> you so much that He sent His <u>Son</u> to die on a <u>cross</u> for You. It is because Jesus <u>rose</u> from the dead that you are saved from your sins.

PRACTICE

If I practice, I'll get better at what I want to do.

Therefore, prepare your minds for action.
– 1 Peter 1:13

Practice Makes Perfect

"Keep going," Mommy said as Evan hacked at the hard ground with his small shovel.

"I don't think I can do it," Evan said, grunting as he tried to push the shovel into the dirt again and again.

"Sure you can," Mommy said, "you just have to learn how to do it. It just takes practice."

Mommy took the shovel from Evan and showed him how to hold it so that it went into the ground easier. After a few more tries, Evan was able to dig more easily.

"I can do it! I can do it!" Evan yelled as his pile of dirt grew bigger and bigger. Before he knew it, he had dug a very big hole just the right size in which to plant a new flower.

Evan had trouble digging at first, but he soon learned how to do it because he kept trying. In the same way, if you practice at being good and doing only the things that God wants, you will get better at being a Christian. Remember: practice makes perfect!

Your Turn

1. Can you think of something that you got better at because you kept practicing?

_____

_____

2. Why is it important to practice at being a Christian?

_____

_____

Prayer

God, please help me to remember that I need to practice at being a Christian all the time. Amen.

NEW PLANT

Read this to your child: "God wants you to practice because the more you practice, the better you will get at the things you need to do. If you practice enough, you'll be really good at coloring. Finish coloring the picture below. Be careful to stay between the lines!"

SECRECY

I should admit when I'm wrong.

He will guide you into all truth.
– John 16:13

Lemonade Secrets

Oh, no, thought Hayden. He had been drinking a can of soda in the back seat of the van, and it had spilled. Where there was once a half-can of soda, now there was none. Daddy was going to be so, so mad!

Hayden could feel his legs and bottom were all wet from the sticky soda. He knew he should tell Daddy what happened, but he was afraid of getting in trouble, so Hayden decided to keep it a secret.

As time went by, Hayden's tummy and head hurt because he felt so bad for keeping the secret. When Daddy finally stopped the car and discovered what had happened, Hayden was almost happy the truth was out. He just wanted his secret to be over so he could feel better.

After Daddy cleaned up the mess, he told Hayden that he would be punished by not being allowed to drink soda in the van again.

"But you are not being punished for the mess, because that was an accident," said Daddy. "You are being punished for keeping it a secret."

Everyone makes mistakes sometimes, but that's not important. What is important is what you do about those mistakes. God wants you to admit when you're wrong, not keep it a secret. After all, God always knows everything anyway. You can't keep a secret from Him!

Your Turn

1. Have you ever kept a "bad" secret?

_____

_____

2. Why does God want you to admit when you're wrong?

_____

_____

Prayer

God, please help me to remember that You know everything. I should admit when I'm wrong and not keep secrets. Amen.

WHEN TO TELL MOM OR DAD

Read this to your child: "Some secrets are bad to keep. God wants you to tell Mommy or Daddy when bad things happen. Below are some pictures of things that have happened to Hayden. Draw a circle around the ones that he should tell his mommy."

REWARDS

I don't need to be rewarded for doing good things.

God loves a cheerful giver.

– 2 Corinthians 9:7

Feeling Rewarded

"Why did he do that?" asked Antonio, holding the dollar bill in his hand. "I told him he didn't have to pay me."

Antonio was helping hand out popcorn at the church fair. The popcorn was free, but a man had insisted on giving Antonio some money anyway.

"He said I was doing a really good job," Antonio told Mommy.

"I guess he just wanted you to know how much he liked what you were doing," said Mommy. "I think he wanted you to have a reward for being such a good boy."

"But I didn't need to be given anything. I would have done it anyway," said Antonio. "It's fun."

Rewards can be money, toys or any number of things...but the best reward is knowing that you're doing what God wants. Antonio was helping his church by handing out popcorn. He didn't need a reward for that. His reward was knowing he was being a good boy for God.

Your Turn

1. What kinds of things do you do to help without being rewarded?

_____

_____

2. What could you do to help at your church as Antonio was?

_____

_____

Prayer

God, please help me to remember that I don't need to be rewarded for being good and helping others. Amen.

FAVORITE REWARDS

Read this to your child: "You don't need to be rewarded for doing good things. Knowing that you're doing what God wants should be reward enough. But sometimes you get rewards without asking. Antonio's favorite reward is below. What is your favorite reward? Draw a picture of it in the box (turn the book sideways first)."

HONESTY

I should be nice and keep my bad thoughts to myself.

Speaking the truth in love.

– Ephesians 4:15

Yucky Dress

"That dress doesn't look good on you," Brady said to the lady at his play group.

"Oh," said the lady with a frown. "Thanks for telling me." But she wasn't really thankful. She was hurt.

"Brady!" Mommy scolded. "You shouldn't have said that."

"Why not?" Brady asked. "It's true. That dress doesn't look nice. I don't like that dress on her."

"You may think so," Mommy explained, "but it's not okay to say it out loud."

"Why not?" Brady asked.

"Because you hurt her feelings," said Mommy. "Even if something is true, you don't have to always say it, especially if what you think could hurt someone."

It's always good to tell the truth, but that doesn't mean you have to always say the truth out loud. If telling the truth would hurt someone, then it's okay to keep your thoughts to yourself. God wants you to be kind to others, not hurtful.

Your Turn

1. Why did Brady's mommy tell him he shouldn't have said the truth out loud?

_____

_____

2. Have you ever said something that was true but it hurt someone?

_____

_____

Prayer

God, please help me to remember that sometimes I need to keep my thoughts to myself. Amen.

LEARNING THE TRUTH

Read this to your child: "Sometimes you shouldn't say the truth out loud, especially if saying it could hurt someone's feelings. The best way to learn the truth is by reading the Bible. The Bible is the book God gave you to teach you how to live. Below are some things that God gave you to teach you the truth. Finish coloring the pictures and talk about each one with your mommy or daddy."

VANITY

My behavior is more important than how I look.

God does not judge by external appearance.
– Galatians 2:6

Acting Pretty

"No!" screamed Janelle as her mommy brushed her hair. "I want braids!"

"Your hair looks pretty when it's down, too," said her big brother, Scotty, as he watched Mommy walk away.

"No," Janelle continued to holler. "Come back, Mommy. I want braids!"

"We don't have time," said Mommy as she hurried around the room. "We have to leave in five minutes. I don't have time to braid your hair right now."

"But I want to look pretty," Janelle whined as she kicked her feet against the stool on which she was sitting.

"You'd better stop it," Scotty warned his sister. "You're acting really bad. You're going to get in trouble."

Just as Scotty finished his warning, Janelle's stool tipped over, and she crashed to the floor.

Janelle wasn't hurt from falling off the stool, just scared. She had wanted pretty braids so much that she forgot something that is even more important–acting pretty. God cares more about how you look on the inside than how you look on the outside.

Your Turn

1. Do you look as good on the inside as you do on the outside?

_____

_____

2. Why does God care how you act?

_____

_____

Prayer

God, please help me to remember that how I act is more important than how I look. Amen.

WHAT'S PRETTY?

Read this to your child: "God wants you to look good on the inside–that's more important than what kind of clothes you wear or how your hair looks. Can you tell the difference between acting pretty and just looking pretty? Look at the two pictures below. Point out what is 'looking' pretty and what is 'acting' pretty."

INTERPRETATION

God's interpretation is best.

Set your mind on things above.

– Colossians 3:2

The White House

"I like the white house," Matt said as Daddy and he drove down the road.

"Why do you like the White House?" Daddy asked. "Is it because the President lives there?"

"The President lives in the white house?" Matt whispered. "Wow. I didn't know that. The President is our neighbor."

"No, the President isn't our neighbor, Matt," Daddy explained. "He lives far, far away."

"No, he doesn't," Matt insisted. "He lives in the white house."

"Yes, but that's very far from where we live," Daddy said.

"No, it's not," said Matt. "It's right there!"

As Daddy looked to where Matt was pointing, he noticed that they were at the corner of their road where there was a white house!

"That's the white house," said Matt. "I always know that we're almost home when I see it."

Matt thought the "white house" meant one thing, while his daddy thought it meant another. Everyone sees things a little differently based on their experiences. You can know how God sees things by reading the Bible. The best way to interpret things is God's way.

Your Turn

1. What is the difference between Matt's white house and his daddy's?

_____

_____

2. How can you know how God sees things?

_____

_____

Prayer

God, please help me to learn to see things Your way. Amen.

DIFFERENT THINGS
DIFFERENT USES

Read this to your child: "God's way is the best way, even though there are many ways to interpret what you see. Look at the pictures below and draw a line from each picture on the left to the different things it could be used for on the right."

AVERSION

I should do what God wants me to do.

Trust in the Lord forever.

– Isaiah 26:4

Yucky, Yummy Broccoli

"I don't like it!" yelled Danny. "I don't want it."

Danny had been given a big piece of broccoli with his dinner. He didn't want to eat it.

Mommy looked Danny straight in the eye and explained, "I only gave you one piece, and you've eaten broccoli before, so it's not too much for me to expect you to eat it. You need it to grow big and strong."

Danny looked down at his plate. He didn't want to eat his broccoli, but he didn't want Mommy to be mad at him either. What could he do?

As Mommy hurried around the kitchen, Danny decided that he would just drop his broccoli on the floor. "Oops," he said as he watched the green vegetable fall to the floor under the table.

Now he wouldn't have to eat something that he didn't like, he thought. But Mommy just washed it off and put it back on his plate!

Something can be good for you even if you don't like it. Danny didn't like broccoli, but it was good for him so he should have eaten it. God wants you to do what's best for you, even if you sometimes don't want to do it. Don't just do what you like to do...do what God wants you to do.

Your Turn

1. Have you ever eaten something you didn't like just because it was good for you?

   _____

   _____

2. Why should you do what's good for you even if you don't want to?

   _____

   _____

Prayer

God, please help me to do the things that are best for me, even if I sometimes don't like those things. Amen.

HEALTHY LIVING

Read this to your child: "God knows what's best for you. Even if you don't like something, you should do it anyway if God says you should. Below are some things you should do and some you shouldn't do. Draw an X through the ones you shouldn't do. Talk with Mommy or Daddy about why these things are good or bad for you."

DEDICATION

I should do what I say I will do.

Let your light shine.
– Matthew 5:16

Will's Walking Group

"I don't want to go walking anymore," said Will. His play group had been taking walks around the block each day. He thought it was fun at first, but now he wanted to quit.

"You said you wanted to go walking with the group," said Mommy. "Why don't you want to do it anymore?"

"It takes too long," answered Will. "I want to play on the playground instead of just walking."

"But that's not as good for you," Mommy said. "And don't forget, you already told Mrs. Peterson that you would walk with the group each week, so she's counting on you."

"But I don't want to!" Will shouted. "I want to play!"

Will didn't want to keep walking, even though he had told Mrs. Peterson he would. His mommy told him he had to keep walking with the group, at least for a few times, because it was the right thing to do. He needed to show some dedication.

God wants you to stick with the things you say you'll do. Don't say you'll do something, and then try to get out of it. Show dedication in all you do, especially when going to church and learning more about God.

Your Turn

1. Have you ever tried to quit something after you joined?

_____

_____

2. Why is it important to stick with something?

_____

_____

Prayer

God, please help me to remember that I should always do the things I say I'll do. Amen.

PLAYGROUND MAZE

Read this to your child: "God wants you to do the things you say you're going to do. You can help Will walk to his playground, but be careful. Don't let Will get distracted along the way."

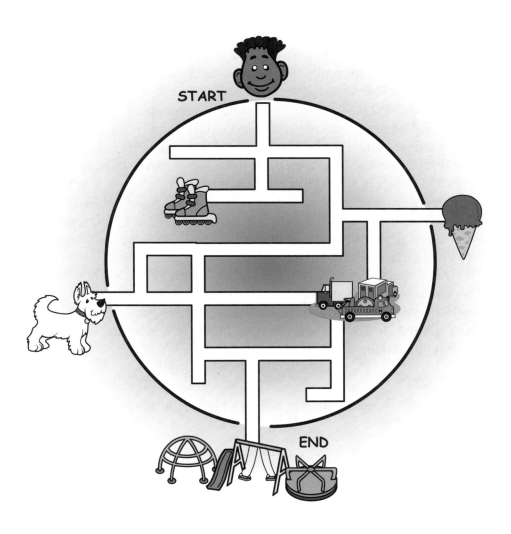

SELF-DISCIPLINE

I should make myself do the right thing.

Never tire of doing what is right.
– 2 Thessalonians 3:13

Sleepy Hayden

"I'm too tired," Hayden murmured as Mommy nudged him awake.

"Come on," said Mommy, "it's time to get up for church."

Hayden knew he should get up, but he was so tired! His eyes slowly started to close, and it felt good. It would be so nice to go back to sleep.

But then Hayden wondered what God would think of his skipping church to sleep? Would that make God happy?

Hayden decided he could sleep anytime, but he could only go to church right then. He knew God would want him to be there. So even though it was difficult, Hayden forced himself to get up out of bed.

When Mommy came back a few minutes later, she was surprised to see that Hayden was dressed and making his bed. Not only did Hayden please God, he had also made his mommy happy!

It's not always easy to do the right thing. Mommy or Daddy won't always be around to tell you what to do. Sometimes you have to make yourself do what is right. Hayden knew God and his parents wanted him to go to church. He knew it was the right thing for him to do. What right things can you decide to do?

Your Turn

1. Do you remember a time when you did the right thing even though it was hard to do?

_____

_____

2. Why is going to church important?

_____

_____

Prayer

God, please help me to do what You would want me to do, even when it's hard. Amen.

WHAT HAYDEN LIKES

Read this to your child: "You should do what God wants you to do, even if it's not easy. Hayden likes going to church, even though it's not always easy to do. Below is something else Hayden likes. Can you guess what it is? Just color in the spaces that have the letter 'A' in them and you'll soon find out."

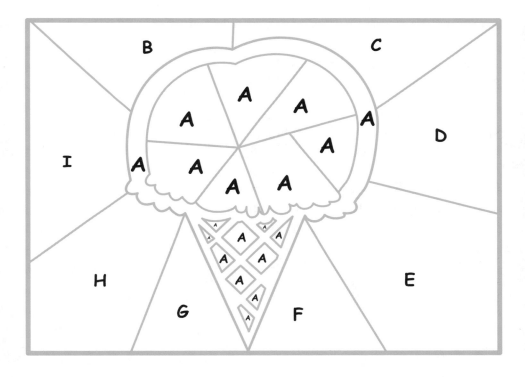

ASSUMPTIONS

I should get all the facts before I think someone is lying.

Do not testify against your neighbor without cause.
– Proverbs 24:28

Suspicious Smell

"Whose perfume were you spraying?" Mommy asked when Joey got home. He had been visiting Sam, and now he smelled like perfume.

"No one," answered Joey.

Mommy held Joey close and sniffed. "I know you were spraying perfume because I can smell it," she said.

"I wasn't spraying perfume!" insisted Joey.

Mommy didn't ask about it again…until the next time Joey went to Sam's. Once again, when he got home Joey smelled like perfume, but he still insisted that he had not been spraying it.

Some time later, Mommy heard Joey say he liked visiting with his friend because they got to play with shaving cream.

"A-ha," Mommy laughed to herself. "Joey had been telling the truth. He didn't smell like perfume after his visits–he smelled like shaving cream!"

Mommy thought Joey was using perfume because of how he smelled. She was wrong. Before you decide that someone is lying to you, you should have good reasons. God does not want you to think poorly of someone without the facts. Get the information first, then decide what you will do.

Your Turn

1. Have you ever thought someone was lying, only to find out later that you were wrong?

_____

_____

2. Why is it important to get all the facts before you think someone is lying?

_____

_____

Prayer

God, please help me to remember that I shouldn't think someone is lying unless I have good reasons to do so. Amen.

ODORS

Read this to your child: "God doesn't want you to accuse someone of lying unless you're sure of it. Joey's mommy shouldn't have accused him of lying just because he smelled good. Draw a line from the smiley face to the things that smell good. Draw a line from the frowning face to the things that don't smell good. Circle the picture of the smell you like best."

PRESERVATION

I need to take good care of all of God's creations.

For by him all things were created.

– Colossians 1:16

Scary Orb Spider

Nick was scared when he saw it, but he couldn't help getting closer. He had never seen a spider that was so big or so pretty. The spider had a round, yellow body with long, black legs, and it held itself very still.

As Nick watched, his daddy told him that the spider was called an orb spider. When the spider started to move, Nick jumped back.

"Stomp it," he said, grabbing onto Daddy's leg for comfort.

"Don't worry," Daddy said, "it won't come after you. It has to stay in its web or it will fall to the ground."

Nick didn't care if he was safe or if the spider was pretty...he was still scared, and he wanted the spider gone.

When they got into the house, Daddy told Nick more about the orb spider and why it's important to have spiders. He told Nick how spiders eat lots of bugs and how they're an important part of nature.

God gives you a wonderful world, and He wants you to take good care of that world. Some of the things God made may seem scary to you. But that doesn't mean you should stomp them. Everything, even orb spiders, are part of God's world.

Your Turn

1. Are there things in nature that you don't like?

_____

_____

2. Why is it important to take care of God's world?

_____

_____

Prayer

God, please help me to remember that I should take care of all the things in nature that You have created. Amen.

NEWSPAPER TENT

Read this to your child: "God wants you to take good care of all that He created. One way to take care of things is by not being wasteful. Use newspaper in a new way by making this newspaper tent."

What You Need

old newspapers

tape

What to Do

1. Stack several layers of newspapers and tightly roll them lengthwise.

2. Secure the rolls with tape.

3. Make nine rolls (these will make the frame of the house).

4. Make a triangle shape with three of the rolls, taping them together.

5. Make another triangle with three more rolls.

6. Position the triangles opposite each other and connect the top point with another roll.

7. Connect the bottom points with a roll on each side.

8. With single sheets of newspaper, you can now cover the sides of your frame to finish your tent.

REPENTANCE

I shouldn't ask for forgiveness unless I am sorry.

People should repent.
– Mark 6:12

Sorry

"Henry called me a bad name!" Grace called from her room.

Grace and her brother, Henry, had been playing blocks together in her room. But Henry got mad when she accidentally knocked over his building.

"Well, she's being mean," Henry called to Mommy.

"Now, Henry, you know it's wrong to call people bad names," Mommy scolded as she entered the room.

Henry looked both sad and angry. "I know," he said.

"Then don't you think you should say you're sorry?" asked Mommy.

Henry looked at Grace, took a deep breath and said, "Sorry."

Henry and Grace started playing again. But a few minutes later, Mommy heard Grace yell, "Henry's calling me bad names again!"

Being sorry isn't just words, it means you will try not to make the same mistake again. Henry said he was sorry, but he didn't really mean it because he called his sister another bad name just a few minutes later.

You can tell God you're sorry when you do something bad and He will forgive you. But it is up to you to see that you do not do the same bad thing again. Don't ask for forgiveness unless you really mean it.

Your Turn

1. Have you ever said you were sorry when you didn't really mean it?

_____

_____

2. Why is it wrong to ask for forgiveness if you are not sorry?

_____

_____

Prayer

God, please help me to remember that I should really mean it when I say I'm sorry. Amen.

GOD POCKET

Read this to your child: "God wants you to say you're sorry when you do something wrong, but He also wants you to mean it. Here's an activity that can help remind you how God wants you to live."

What You Need

construction paper

crayons

scissors

tape

What to Do

1. Cut out a double pocket shape as shown in the illustration below.

2. Fold the pocket where shown at the dashed line.

3. Tape the sides and bottom.

4. Decorate the pocket with crayons.

5. Cut some small squares of paper (the right size to fit into the pocket).

6. On each square, draw a picture of different biblical messages (such as each of the Ten Commandments).

7. Each morning pick another message from the pocket.

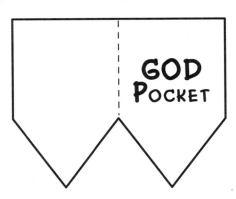

CHRISTLIKENESS

I should show my love for Jesus.

Set them an example by doing what is good.

– Titus 2:7

The Jesus Grandma

"Which grandma's house are we going to?" Sam asked.

Sam and his sisters were going to Grandma's house while Mommy and Daddy went to a meeting.

"Is it the regular grandma or the Jesus grandma?" he asked.

"Why do you call her the 'Jesus grandma'?" Mommy asked, smiling.

Sam thought about it for a moment, then answered, "Because the Jesus grandma prays and talks about Jesus a lot."

As Sam thought some more he added, "And Jesus grandma's Christmas tree has ornaments about Jesus on it!"

"Why do you think Jesus grandma talks about Jesus so much?" Mommy asked.

"Because she loves Jesus very much," Sam answered as he went to play.

Sam's grandma showed her love for Jesus in many ways. She talked about Jesus and prayed to Jesus. Sam knew his grandma loved Jesus because he could see her love for Him.

Jesus wants people to be able to see your love for Him. Do the things Jesus would want you to do, and teach others about Him. Then you will be like Jesus grandma!

Your Turn

1. Why did Sam call his grandma "Jesus Grandma"?

_____

_____

2. What are some ways that you show your love for Jesus?

_____

_____

Prayer

Jesus, please help me to always behave like Jesus grandma, so that people can see my love for You. Amen.

SYMBOLS OF LOVE

Read this to your child: "Jesus wants you to show your love for Him. Below is a picture of Sam's bedroom. Can you circle all the things that show Sam's love for Jesus? (Turn the book sideways to see the picture better."

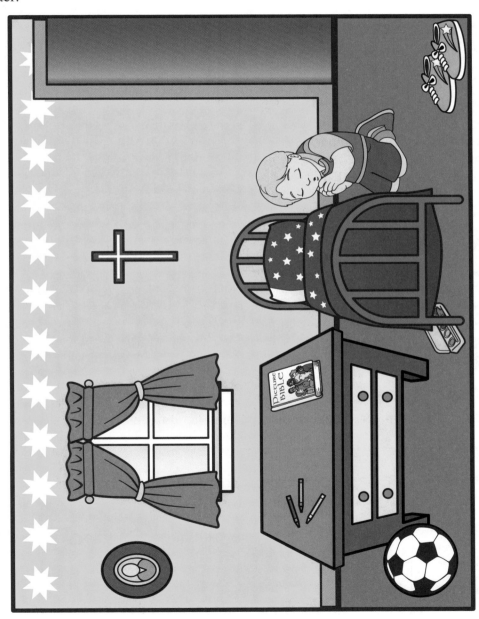

REDEMPTION

I am saved only by my love for Jesus.

He saved us...because of his mercy.

– Titus 3:5

What Matters Most

"I want to help," said Kevin.

Mommy was helping the church get ready for their annual fair. There was lots to do.

"Let me help!" Kevin cried again. "I really, really want to help!"

"How come you always want to help?" Mommy asked. She knew Kevin was a good helper, but she wasn't sure why he liked it so much.

"I want to go to heaven," said Kevin. "I'm going to do lots of good things, and that way I'll get to go to heaven someday."

"That's not how you get to heaven," said Mommy.

"It's not?" Kevin asked.

"No," explained Mommy. "Jesus likes it when you do good things, but you can go to heaven someday just by believing in Him. That's what matters most."

It's nice to do good things, but it is your love for Jesus that is most important. To go to heaven, all you have to do is tell Jesus you love Him, say you're sorry for any bad things you've done and ask Him to help you live your life. If you are ready to do that, ask your mommy or daddy to pray with you.

Your Turn

1. Can Kevin get to heaven just by doing good things?

_____

_____

2. Do you do good things? Why?

_____

_____

Prayer

Jesus, please help me to remember that doing good things is wonderful, but it is by believing in You that I will someday go to heaven. Amen.

BELIEVING IN JESUS

Read this to your child: "If you want to go to heaven someday, believe in and love Jesus. Below is a picture for you to finish coloring."